Front Cover Photo

It's 1950 at the Raceland, Kentucky, Carshops and the C&O photographer has the paint shop boys carefully posed for this publicity shot. Metal stencils, such as the ones displayed by these C&O painters, produce clean crisp lettering. The clock was ticking on the red paint scheme, though. Seven years later the painters' guns would be filled with Signal Yellow paint. *C&O Photo, C&OHS Collection*

STEEL CABOOSES
OF THE
CHESAPEAKE & OHIO
1937 - 2010

Copyright © 2010 by Dwight Jones

All rights reserved.
No portion of this book may be reproduced without the written permission of the author, except for brief extracts published as part of a review.

Library of Congress Control Number: 2010912621
International Standard Book Number 978-0-9715476-5-0

Published by

B&O Caboose Publishers
Linking 13 Great Books with the Nation

Columbus, Ohio

Printed by
Walsworth Publishing Co.
Marceline, MO 64658

Contents

Introduction 3

C&O / PM Caboose Summary 8

1. Hocking Valley Steel Caboose 10
2. Pere Marquette Coach Cabooses 13
3. Pere Marquette A901 Series 15
4. Pere Marquette A950 Series 20
5. Troop Sleepers 25
6. C&O 90000 Series 29
7. C&O 90050 Series 36
8. C&O 90200 Series 42
9. C&O 90300 Series 49
10. Experimental Conversions 55
11. C&O 90350 Series 63
12. Extended Vision Cabooses 68
13. C&O 3500/3600 Series 82
14. C&O Bay-window Cabooses 90
15. Toledo Terminal Cabooses 99
16. Safety Cabooses 107
17. Careful Car Handling Cabooses 115
18. Solar Cabooses 119
19. Painting and Lettering 122
20. Caboose Trucks 131

Caboose Totals by Year 134

21. Caboose Markers 135

Notes 139

C&O/B&O/WM 1987, 2010 Caboose Summary 142

Acknowledgments 143

C&O Cabooses in Color 146

C&O caboose 903248, from the class of '69, brings up the markers on a seemingly endless string of CPOX (Consumers' Power) rotary-dump gondolas leaving Columbus, Ohio, for Russell, Kentucky, on February 12, 1983. To the C&O crew, it's just another "Chicken Pox" train. *Dwight Jones*

Steel Cabooses of the Chesapeake & Ohio

Introduction

The introduction to the original volume, completed in January 1986, provided an overall look at the contents of the book as well as a synopsis of the C&O caboose fleet at that time. That history is still pertinent today and therefore much of that original introduction is reproduced below.

Books on specialized railroad equipment, locomotives excluded, are rare on the library shelves of railroad historians. Those that have been published generally introduce themselves with a common theme, that railroad historians/ photographers have concentrated their efforts on motive power almost exclusively and to the detriment of other types of railroad equipment. The result is that there is little photographic coverage of early types of non-locomotive rolling stock.

Secondly, there seems to be a great lack of hard-core historical data—both drawings and roster entries. Sometimes railroads are reluctant to allow outsiders to search their files, for a variety of reasons. In other instances the old, outdated files have been destroyed to make room for new materials. The situation has been further aggravated by mergers and megamergers.

Books that deal with cabooses are very rare, even among treatments of rolling stock. Fortunately, Chesapeake & Ohio steel cabooses have fared better than many other pieces of equipment, both in photographic coverage and technical data. Veteran railfan photographers such as Paul Dunn were recording cabooses on film while others concentrated on locomotives. The C&O has not only preserved much needed historical documentation, but has been generous in allowing historians access to those materials. Much material also has been presented to the C&O Historical Society for preservation and cataloging.

In the pages that follow, effort has been concentrated on bringing together a vast amount of data and technical material to document, as thoroughly as possible, the history of C&O's steel caboose fleet. Each group of cabooses is presented to the reader with historical text, diagram sheet, extensive photo coverage, and a detailed roster compilation. [the roster will be published as a separate publication at a future date-dj] Specialized chapters and appendices have been included to cover some of the more interesting caboose developments, such as "Careful Car Handling", "Solar", and "Safety" cabooses.

Painting and lettering, a subject that many modelers would rate at the top of their list in importance, has received extensive coverage. In addition to a chapter on the subject, representative photographs throughout this book have been identified with a code placed at the end of the photo caption that grades the caboose paint and lettering scheme: (STD)—

The Transportation Department in Baltimore played a constant game of checkers, moving cabooses around the system based on freight patterns and traffic flow. Deadhead moves, which are both costly and unproductive, were a last resort. Sometimes they were unavoidable. In this photo, cabooses are being deadheaded to Columbus from Russell, Kentucky, on train HV-95, March 6, 1983. *Dwight Jones*

And what happened to these four cabs? A private owner near Hagerstown acquired the 3182, scrappers got 3646 and 3116, and a private owner in northern Ohio has the 3248.

As caboose maintenance was reduced, bad-ordered cars accumulated at selected system locations. Far more cars could be found at the Grand Rapids, Michigan, shops than at any other locale. When this photo was taken on September 5, 1983, nearly 60 cabooses were in heavy bad-order storage there. And that's not counting the in-service cabooses and those awaiting light repair! *Dwight Jones*

standard paint and lettering scheme; (NON-STD)—nonstandard paint and lettering scheme. It is hoped that these will be of great help to modelers who seek to paint and letter their models accurately.

The roster sections are the most extensive ever published on caboose cars. Some may question the need for such extensive rosters. "Who cares when and where sanitary toilets are installed?" they may ask. On the surface, that may appear to be a valid question. However, there is much more to be learned from this type of entry. It gives insight into government mandates that required such modifications, it helps determine which system shops were assigned to do certain work, and it lets those discriminating modelers who model certain regions of the railroad easily determine which cabooses were assigned to the geographic region they model, and number their cars accordingly. [most rosters have been removed from the 2010 edition and will be published in the future as a separate publication-dj]

For those who care to take the time to study them, the rosters will be found to contain a wealth of information. Be sure to study the section on roster interpretation, which explains many of the abbreviations and codes used in the roster sections. One part of the roster that is perhaps unique is the 1983 system location of every C&O caboose left in existence at that time. This information offers valuable insight into the distribution of the caboose fleet across the vast C&O system.[1] The year 1983 was one of the last years that C&O cabooses were still at home. In the years that followed they began showing up more and more on Baltimore & Ohio lines as the Transportation Department worked to truly integrate the pooled cabooses of the two roads.

One chapter covers a group of Troop Sleepers that were acquired from the government by the C&O and were converted for a number of different uses, including using some of the cars as cabooses. They did not last long in that service and no photos of the cars as cabooses have surfaced.

The past several years have been very interesting for me, as I have traveled around the system photographing and observing the operation of C&O cabooses. The travels took me through every state and into every yard still frequented by C&O. I observed the delivery of the new C&O baywindow cabooses, the retirement of the last few wooden cabooses, and then the gradual retirement of older steel cabooses.

By the mid-1980s, the handwriting was on the wall—cabooses were a threatened species. End-of-train devices (EOTs) appeared on selected manifests, later spread to Trailer Trains, then more manifests, then long-distance coal trains.

The economies were overwhelming, For the price of a caboose battery (about $5000) the railroad could purchase one EOT. Then came the big savings: switching costs and maintenance! Clearly, the caboose didn't stand a chance. Except, that is, on the Virginia Division. The Commonwealth of Virginia is one of the few states in the nation that has a mandatory caboose law (others are Montana, Oregon, Nebraska, and New Mexico). As railroads build more and more documentation on the safe operation of trains using EOTs, it will be only a matter of time until mandatory caboose laws are repealed.

As more and more end-of-train devices go into service (137 units were owned by Chessie in late January 1986), more and more cabooses become obsolete. So far Chessie has been cautious—there have been no mass retirements of C&O cabooses. Instead, the railroad has chosen simply to stop all major repair work on the cars. As cabooses are "bad ordered" and the repair estimate exceeds a specified number of hours, the cabs are simply put into storage. In late January 1986, 325 system cabooses were in heavy bad-order status—that's about 28 percent of the fleet! Long strings of bad-ordered C&O, B&O, and Western Maryland cabooses have accumulated at such system locations as Chicago, Grand Rapids, Russell, Willard, Cumberland, Hagerstown, Elkins, Huntington, and Clifton Forge. If they're needed they can be repaired and returned to service. Likely they won't be.

As for the future of the caboose, it may not be bright, but it should certainly be interesting. What will happen to the large number of steel cabooses left? Will they become backyard playhouses or take up display service in parks with steam locomotives? Will states such as Virginia eliminate mandatory caboose laws, or will the unions succeed in lobbying other state legislatures to pass similar caboose protection laws? With maintenance requirements reduced, it is clear that those cabooses that do survive will become more and more drab as caboose painting becomes as obsolete as boiler inspections on steam locomotives.

I hope you will enjoy the following pages as much as I have enjoyed assembling them. Perhaps when you are finished, you, too, may want to join the small (but growing) ranks of the caboose aficionado! Happy reading.

Introduction Supplement January 2010

It has been 24 years since the above introduction was penned for the first edition. It is interesting to look back at that history now and see just how much of our glass-ball speculation actually has come true.

A lot has happened during the past two decades. Virginia Governor Gerald Baliles signed legislation on Monday, February 22, 1988, repealing Virginia's mandatory caboose law. The repeal became effective July 1. Virginia, the first state requiring cabooses, also was to be the last. Montana also had a mandatory caboose law, but a Federal Court ruled that it no longer could be enforced.

Of course the biggest change has been in the selling off of the C&O caboose fleet—both to scrappers and to private owners. We have stayed on top of this, and have updated our rosters to show final dispositions for all of those hundreds of cabooses that have been sold.

Deliberately, photo coverage of CSX-painted cars has been kept to a bare minimum in this updated publication. A future book will be published that covers the history of CSX cabooses from the start of the CSX era. We have made an on-going effort to stay up to date with all cabooses on CSX and record that history as it happens, including substantial research trips and photography of repaints.

A major decision that was needed for this revised edition was whether to cover all of the Troop Sleepers that were included in the first edition. After discussion with many of our C&O fan contacts, it was decided only to cover those Troop Sleepers which actually became cabooses.

Most of the "display" cabooses also have been removed for this updated edition. C&O display cabooses now can be found in other books which are shown on page 144—no need to duplicate the coverage here.

When this book on C&O steel cabooses first was published in 1987, we suspected that we would receive some further clarifications on various aspects of the subject after the book was published, distributed, and reviewed by others who

Loads west, empties east. Conductors will exchange salutations as their class C-15C and C-25 cabooses pass at Greenlawn Avenue in Columbus, Ohio, on July 17, 1982. With the expanded use of end-of-train devices, this scene would become increasingly difficult to duplicate. *Dwight Jones*

might have insight into specifics not covered by the book. We also knew that there would be future changes to the C&O caboose fleet–mostly in the form of cars being sold, donated, or scrapped–and that dedicated C&O and caboose enthusiasts would want to stay abreast of these updates.

It's indeed rare that an update to a previously published book is completed that addresses those issues just mentioned. Carl Shaver's C&O diesel review book and his 1937 C&O freight car book are among the few that we can think of (both published by the C&O Historical Society). In the "Acknowledgments" section of the C&O caboose book it was mentioned that it was our intention to keep this book updated, probably with yearly addendum sheets. With time needed to pursue other projects, the idea of yearly addendum sheets proved impractical. Instead, a more workable solution seemed to be to issue corrections, updates, and additions after several years, with a complete republication. This is the first of those efforts.

We would like to thank the many individuals who have taken the time to supply additional facts or expand upon some point made in the original text–and to keep us abreast of various C&O caboose news that they have observed around the system. Although we certainly make the effort to do so, it is indeed difficult for one individual to keep up to date with caboose happenings across the large CSX system. So keep those cards, emails, letters and phone calls coming in with reports on any B&O, C&O or WM caboose news that you learn about. We are very proud of the fact that our rosters contain final dispositions for approximately 500 C&O cabooses–an incredible number by any standard. Nevertheless, we suspect that a few have dropped through the cracks. We would like to know about those for future updates.

During the Chessie years we had built a substantial and productive network of contacts on the railroad that kept us informed of caboose changes almost as they happened. Each month, for over a decade, a package arrived from Baltimore corporate offices with all caboose changes for the previous month, including retirements, sales, donations, etc. This allowed us to follow up quickly with owners or organizations who had acquired cabooses, or with scrappers who soon would be cutting up a particular car. When CSX was formed these contacts were almost all transferred or took job buyouts or chose retirement. In addition, many of the ways that information flowed on the railroad was changed once CSX consolidations took place and new systems were implemented. The age-old railroad tradition of recording all that happened to equipment so that it would be available was rethought by a new railroad management. Do we really need to record and keep permanently the dates that radios are added to cabooses? Or that toilets are installed? The answer was no. The new mentality was to record certain information on computer databases, then have that information erased from memory after a specified period of time. Computer memory is expensive.

It's been a difficult task keeping up with C&O/B&O/WM cabooses during these modern CSX times. But we have worked hard to develop new contacts and learn about the many computer systems available that contain information. And we have learned that we had better extract and save that computer data before the memory is wiped clean (which sometimes happens after only a few months). Therefore, after an initial struggle, we have been able to maintain continuity for our C&O/B&O/WM caboose records including sales, donations, and other changes. We sympathize with the younger historian, however, who someday will want to

EOT (End of Train) devices came in a variety of shapes and sizes in the mid-1980s. As of mid-October 1987, CSX owned 807 such units, with 22 more on order. Plans were also in the works to order additional quantities. An occasional problem with a caboose marker light caused an EOT to be mounted to a caboose such as depicted in this photo taken at Parsons Yard, Columbus, Ohio, on August 5, 1987. *Dwight Jones*

Representative of the hundreds of C&O steel cabooses scrapped over the past several years is 903127, shown at Columbus, Ohio, August 9, 1992, in the process of being cut up by a private scrap contractor. Many cars were shipped off to scrap yards for scrap processing, while a few, which mostly had mechanical problems which prevented movement on their own wheels, were held locally for cut-up by roving scrap dealers. *Dwight Jones*

compile a history of other equipment–the information simply will not be available. The only way to keep up is on a weekly basis. If you fall behind there likely will be gaps in your records.

When we were working on the original edition of this book in the mid-1980s there were 585 C&O steel cabooses left on the roster (January 1987). As we work on this update in January 2010, over 20 years later, only about 10% of those cars still remain in some type of service on CSX. Although most of the cars that have been removed from the roster were sold for scrap, a few were donated or sold to private parties. Certain of the cars sold to scrap companies were resold by those scrappers to private owners. Many of these have been chronicled in the books listed in the back of this book. Originally we had planned to update the extensive rosters that appeared in the first edition and include them in this revision. Instead we have decided not to include those rosters thus providing more pages for photos and historical coverage. The rosters will be updated and made available at some future point as a stand-alone publication. The separate publication of the rosters will allow them to be updated more often that if they appeared in this work.

The company has used many scrappers to reduce the caboose fleet during the CSX era. In some cases, cabooses are routed to scrap dealers who maintain their own scrap yards where disassembling railroad cars can be accomplished quickly and efficiently. This is the railroad's first choice for scrap cars because cars delivered directly to a scrap facility command a higher price. In other cases, cars cannot move on their own wheels due to mechanical defects, and the company must sell these cars locally. These cars bring less

money because scrap crews must travel to the car, bringing all of their necessary equipment to cut up the car, pay expenses for their crews to stay locally, then truck out the scrap.

Scrap companies with major yards include Mansbach Metal (Ashland, KY), Progress Rail (Albertville, AL), D.J. Joseph (Wilder, KY), Louisville Scrap (Louisville, KY), Brock Scrap (Cumberland, MD), Steel Processing (Albertville, AL), Hickory Steel (Birmingham, AL), 183 Scrap (Chicago), Salvage 13 (Savannah, GA), and Mindlin Company (Chicago). (Progress Rail purchased Steel Processing in June 1993, and prior to that, Steel Processing had purchased Hickory Steel in the late 1980s/early 1990s.) Certain of these companies also have mobile crews, which travel around the system cutting up a few cars at one location then move on to the next assignment. Other scrappers which are mostly of the mobile type include Charlie Herman, K&M Recycling, Duraway & Wells, Shorty's Scrap, Davidson Lumber, and Southern Metals.

Special thanks is due Phil Shuster, who supplied several very interesting personal stories from his days of railroad employment. John Riddle also supplied some interesting comments from his years in C&O management. Too bad John did not live to see this update completed.

Dwight Jones
Columbus, Ohio
January 2010

C&O / PM CABOOSE SUMMARY

Series	RR	Old Class	New Class	Date Built	Builder	QTY	Body Type	Notes	Remarks
A15 - A17	C&O					3	Wood		ex M&NE 15-17 (ex PM A359, A379, A615)
A227-A599	PM			1886-1922	**	?	Wood		A227-A251 were four-wheelers
A600-A630	PM			1923-1929	PM Shops	?	Wood		
A700-A702	PM			1924	PM Shops	3	Wood		
A800-A824	PM		C-10	1930	Magor Car	25	Wood		
A901-A925	PM		C-14	1937	Magor Car	25	Steel		
A950-A989	PM		C-16	1941	St. Louis Car	40	Steel		
A1100-series	PM			1921	Std. Steel Car	?	Steel		ex-PM 1100-series coaches
A1200-series	PM			1910-1914	Pullman	?	Steel		ex-PM 1200-series coaches
3100-3325	C&O		C-25	1968-1971	International Car	226	Steel		wide-vision cupola cabooses
3500-3684	C&O		C-15C	1937-1947	see original series	185	Steel		rebuilt from 90000-90199 (1969-70)
90000	C&O			1889	Pullman	1	Wood		from pass/bag/mail #429, 12-7-31
90000-90349	C&O			pre-1915	AC&F	?	Wood		
90000-90049	C&O		C-15	1937	Magor Car	50	Steel		
90050-90099	C&O		C-15A	1941	Magor Car	50	Steel		
90100-90149	C&O		C-15A	1941	St. Louis Car	50	Steel		
90150-90199	C&O		C-15A	1947	AC&F	50	Steel		
90200-90299	C&O		C-20	1949	AC&F	100	Steel		
90299-90325	C&O	K3-6		1926	HV Shops	25	Wood	C	ex HV 300-324; to 90603-90635 (1949)
90300-90349	C&O		C-21	1949	AC&F	50	Steel		
90350-90356	C&O		C-13	1936-1940	BS-WM	7	Steel		ex Western Maryland
90326-90369	C&O	K3-7		1913-1920	HV Shops	42	Wood	D	ex HV 337-379; some to 90326-90647 ('49)
90357-90370	C&O		C-5	1918, 1923	Std. Steel Car	14	Wood	E	ex B&O C2600-series
90370-90398	C&O	K3-8		1882-1907	CHV&T, HV Shops	20	Wood	F	ex Hocking Valley 380-399
90400-90655	C&O	K3-1		1885-1923	Note G	256	Wood	G	to 90403-90434 (1950)
90457-90484	C&O			Note K	Pullman	15	Steel		ex Troop Sleepers
90500-90550	C&O			pre-1909	?	?	Wood		
90603-90635	C&O		C-9	1926	HV Shops	25	Wood		from 90299-90325 (1949)
90638-90647	C&O			1915-1917	HV Shops	9	Wood	H	from 90326-90349 (1949)
90650-90653	C&O		C-9	1929	HV Shops	4	Wood	J	from 91000-91024 (1949 or 1950)
90656-90680	C&O	K3-2	C-7	1924	C&O-Huntington	25	Wood		four rebuilt with steel bodies (1956-1959)
90681-90699	C&O		C-8	1929	HV Shops	19	Wood	J	from 91000-91024 (1949 or 1950)
90700-90799	C&O	K3-3	C-8	1924	Std. Steel Car	100	Wood		
90800-90899	C&O	K3-4	C-8	1926	Std. Tank Car	100	Wood		
90900-90999	C&O	K3-5	C-8	1929	HV Shops	100	Wood		
91000-91024	C&O	K3-5		1929	HV Shops	25	Wood	J	to 90650-90653; 90681-90699 (1949 or 1950)
903326	C&O		C-29	1945	Lehigh Valley	1	Steel		ex Toledo Terminal RR 90
903327-903329	C&O		C-29	1950	International Car	3	Steel		ex Toledo Terminal RR 91-93
904094-904159	C&O		C-27A	1980	FGE	66	Steel		only C&O bay-window cabooses

Builder Codes

** = PM; AC&F; Detroit, Lansing & Northern; Chicago & West Michigan RR
Magor Car = Magor Car Corporation, Passaic, New Jersey
St. Louis Car = St. Louis Car Company, St. Louis, Missouri
AC&F = American Car & Foundry, Chicago, Illinois
HV Shops = Hocking Valley Railway Shops, Logan, Ohio
BS-WM = Bethlehem Steel kits assembled by Western Maryland Shops, Hagerstown, Maryland
Std. Steel Car = Standard Steel Car Company, Butler, Pennsylvania
CHV&T = Columbus, Hocking Valley & Toledo Shops, Logan, Ohio
Pullman = Pullman-Standard Car Manufacturing Company, Chicago, Illinois
Std. Tank Car = Standard Tank Car Company, Sharon, PA
International Car = International Car Corporation, Kenton, Ohio
FGE = Fruit Growers Express Company, Alexandria, Virginia

Notes

A   Old C&O class discontinued in 1935.
B   New C&O/B&O (later Chessie) classes initiated in 1970.
C   Quantity of 25 reflects only ex HV cabs described. Two numbers in series 90299-90325 were already assigned at time of renumbering. When renumbered to 90603-90635, eight numbers were skipped which already were assigned to older existing cabooses.
D   Quantity of 42 reflects only HV cabs described. Two numbers in series 90326-90369 already were assigned at time of renumbering. One HV caboose, number 351, was retired prior to renumbering. Series 90326-90369 left in service in 1949 were renumbered to series 90638-90647 (90645 was skipped) to clear the 90300 series for new steel cabooses.
E   Former B&O C2600-series cars acquired by C&O in 1966-67. Series 90363-90370 were relettered back to B&O in 1970-71.
F   Quantity of 20 reflects only ex HV cabs described. Nine numbers in series 90370-90398 already were assigned at time of renumbering.
G   Various cars in 90400 series built by C&O Shops (Huntington), AC&F and Tredegar (Richmond). Cars remaining in service in 1950 (32) were renumbered to 90403-90434.
H   Quantity of 9 reflects only those cars renumbered from series 90326-90349. One number, 90645, not assigned to these cars (see Note D).
J   Cars in series 91000-91024 were renumbered to 90650-90653 and 90681-90699 in 1949 or 1950. New C-9 class appears to have been assigned in error to series 90650-90653. Series 90681-90699 were assigned class C-8 as were other original K3-5 cabooses.
    The renumbering was to clear the 91000 series for new 70-ton welded hoppers built beginning in 1948 by AC&F (C&O 91000-94999).
K   C&O records indicate a 1945 build date for troop cars acquired by C&O. Possibly some of these cars were actually built in 1943, 1944 or 1946.
L   Early C&O caboose history is sketchy. All known series have been listed but an actual summary beginning date cannot be accurately determined

From the Rule Books ...

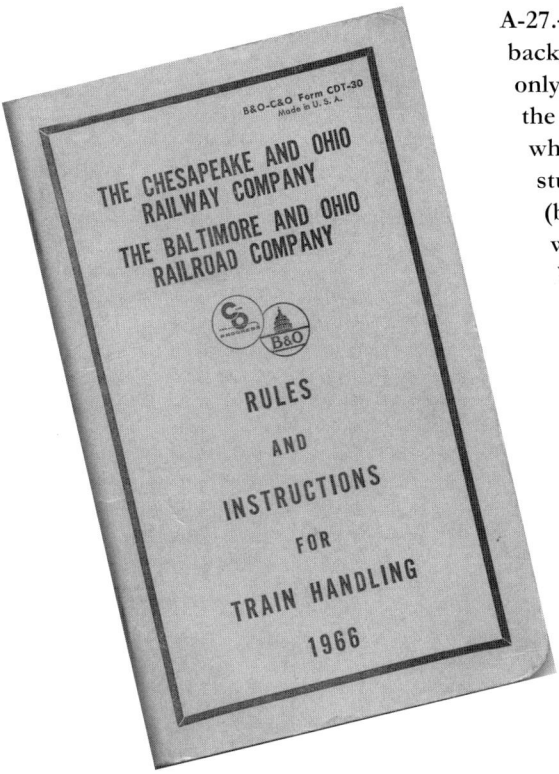

A-27.—Applying Brakes From Rear.—(a) Conductor valves and back-up valves on cabooses are for the purpose of stopping trains only when necessary and must not be used to apply brakes for the purpose of attempting to control slack. Unnecessary use of whistle on caboose platforms is prohibited as this may cause stuck brakes.

(b) Where caboose is equipped with type A-1 caboose valve it will be used for making all service applications from rear. When not in use, handle of A-1 caboose valve to be kept in "Lap" position at extreme left.

A-36.—Caboose Gauge.—The purpose of caboose gauge is to ensure greater safety. Trainmen are responsible for observing gauge to ensure against danger from closed angle cock or low pressure. Where such observations indicate danger they will take necessary precautions such as hand signals, or use of radio, application of hand or air brakes as circumstances warrant.

19. The following signals will be displayed, one on each side of the rear of every train, as markers, to indicate the rear of the train:

Signals Displayed

Equipment	By Day	By Night
Engines and cars not equipped with fixed electric markers	Marker lamps not lighted	Marker lamps lighted showing red to rear.
Engines and cars equipped with fixed electric markers.	Marker lamps lighted showing red to rear	Marker lamps lighted showing red to rear.

1212. Unless otherwise instructed, camp cars, or passenger equipment moved in freight trains must be handled on rear next ahead of the caboose.

1308. Marker lamps must not be carried through any passenger cars when it can be avoided.

Chapter 1

Hocking Valley Steel Caboose

The oldest metal-body caboose to be covered in this book was not built by C&O but by predecessor company Hocking Valley. In April 1926, the Hocking Valley shops at Logan, Ohio, outshopped 25 wood-sheathed caboose cars numbered in HV series 300-324. Built to a C&O system standard design, these were the last caboose cars to be assigned Hocking Valley series road numbers.

Hocking Valley Company builder's photos illustrate car 301 photographed shortly after original construction with wood sheathing, and car 323 with a metal covering applied. From the stenciled data appearing on car 323, it appears that this car was rebuilt with metal sheathing and outshopped in May 1929, about three years after original construction. The difference in the two cars is graphically illustrated by the 3,500-pound weight difference that can be seen in the stenciled weights that appear on each car.

Five months after the metal covering was applied to car 323, the HV shops at Logan started outshopping an order of 125 cabooses for C&O numbered 90900-91024. These were the last cabooses built by the HV shops at Logan and the last wood-sheathed cabooses to be acquired by C&O. One can't help wondering if the application of the metal covering to car 323 was done as an experiment to study application feasibility and cost in preparation for the upcoming lot of 125 cabooses and the possibility of constructing all or part of the 125-car lot in the same manner.

In 1930 HV series 300-324 was renumbered to C&O series 90299-90325 (two older C&O cabooses already occupied two numbers in the series). In 1949 the cars were renumbered, again with other cabooses, to the 90603-series. A roster of what is believed to be the original HV 300-series cabooses has been prepared and is included in this chapter. This roster was prepared from photos and from build dates the railroad had for 90603-series cars. It cannot be concluded that the roster is absolutely correct, due to the absence of critical company renumbering records for the interim road numbers.

In the original edition of this book we indicated it would be nice to have a photo of this special caboose in later years, after

Hocking Valley 323 is shown most likely at the Logan, Ohio, shops after application of metal sheeting on the sides and ends of the body. The cupola retained its wood sheathing on the sides, but may have had metal on the ends. An early practice of mounting a permanent marker to the cupola roof has been maintained, although the marker is moved near one end of the cupola. This marker generally was centered on the cupola. *Phil Shuster Collection*

the C&O renumbering. Unfortunately, no such information or photos were available at that time. Since then we have heard from veteran C&O historian Phil Shuster who supplied a photo of the caboose renumbered as C&O 90635. Company records indicated that the 90635 was destroyed at the Russell Car Shops on November 12, 1954. The records indicated a build date of April 12, 1926. There were no other notes recorded about the fact that the special metal covering had been added.

C&O 90635 was photographed by Phil Shuster at Olentangy, Ohio (northwest side of Columbus), milepost 7.4, as part of a Speno Ballast Cleaner work train in July 1951. Phil indicated that the metal covering on this caboose looked more like sheet metal or tin perhaps applied over the original wood sheathing. The car survived a little over three years after this photo was made. Apparently this caboose spent its last years assigned out of Parsons Yard at Columbus. On this day it was used for MofW crews with 90107 behind it for the freight crew. Likely 90635 was an "extra" cab at Columbus.

Hocking Valley 301 poses as representative of the original configuration of these cars when built new at the HV shops at Logan, Ohio, in April 1926. This car carries a repack date of 12-13-28, an indication that this photo was made after a subsequent shopping. *Phil Shuster Collection*

One of the original HV cars, with wood sheathing, is shown at Toledo, Ohio, on February 15, 1956. It carries small HV initials in the upper right corner. The 90609 was one of the last cars from this group to be retired. *John C. LaRue, Jr. Coll.*

90603-series Roster

No.	Date Built	Date Retired	Disposition
90603	4-24-26	3- -73	Sold 2-7-73 to H. B. Riddleberger, Jr. for $800
90604	4-24-26	11- -63	Destroyed at Russell Carshops 11-13-63
90605	4-24-26	12- -71	Donated 9-24-71 to Handley, WV
90606	4-24-26	12- -71	Sold 10-12-71 to Laro Coal & Iron, Flint, MI, for $600
90608	4-24-26	12- -71	Sold 10-12-71 to Laro Coal & Iron, Flint, MI, for $600
90609	4-24-26	2- -80	Sold 11-7-79 to Portsmouth Iron & Metal; trucks to Raceland
90610	4-24-26	4- -71	Sold 2-22-71 to Mansbach Metal, Ashland, KY
90611	4-24-26	11-21-57	Destroyed: Manhattan Boulevard Terminal
90612	4-24-26	12- -71	Sold 10-12-71 to Laro Coal & Iron, Flint, MI, for $600
90614	4-24-26	7- -71	Leased to B&O 2-19-71; sold 5-25-71 to Staten Island Transportation Railway
90615			No data
90617	4-16-26	11- -83	Put in Limbo at WAL 10-29-81; sold 10-6-82 to Mansbach Metal
90618	4-16-26	11- -82	Put in Dismantle 10-30-81; sold 10-6-82 to Mansbach Metal, Ashland, KY
90619	4-16-26	7- -71	Leased to B&O at Cincinnati 4-16-71; sold 5-25-71 to B&O for $3180.00
90622	4-16-26	11- -75	Sold 11-12-75 to Mary Kay Budak, New Buffalo, MI, for $800
90623	4-12-26	9- -79	Sold 1-18-79 from Huntington to Huntington Metal Salvage
90624	4-12-26	9-4-51	Retired at Walbridge, OH
90626	4-12-26	7- -69	Sold 6-23-69 from Russell, KY, to Patrick Ettien
90629	4-5-26	8- -71	Donated 2-4-71 to Advent Christian Church, Iron Gate, VA
90630	4-5-26	12- -71	Sold 10-1-71 to Alexander Scale Models, Grand Rapids, MI, for $800
90631	4-5-26	7- -71	Leased to B&O 10-9-70, at HTG; sold 5-25-71 to B&O for $3180.00
90634	4-12-26	4- -80	Put in Limbo at Saginaw; sold 3-11-80 to Howard Grube
90635	4-12-26	11-12-54	Destroyed: Russell Carshops
90637	4-5-26	1-25-50	Destroyed: Russell Carshops

Missing C&O numbers in the above roster are believed to have been assigned to "other" types of cabooses

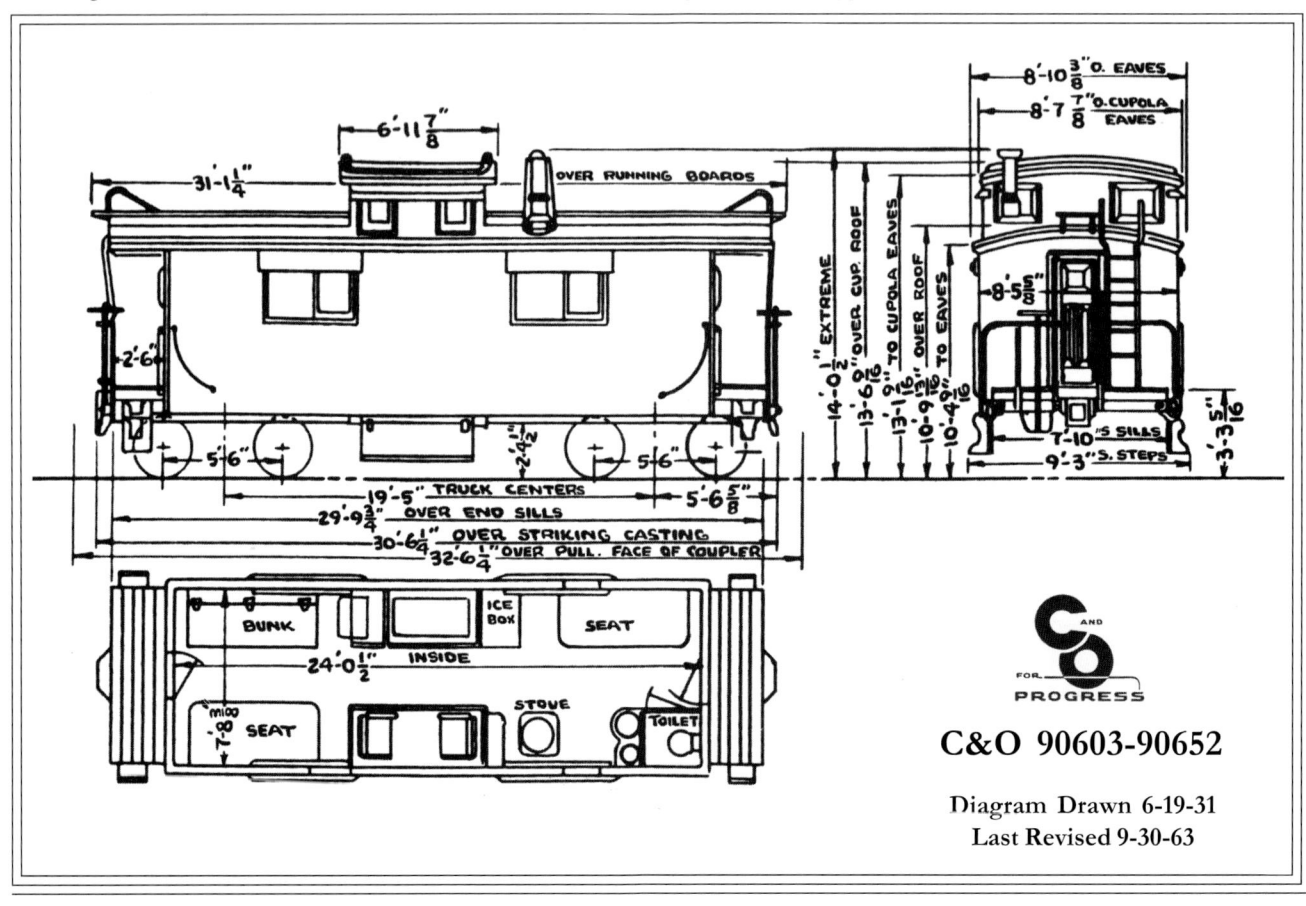

C&O 90603-90652

Diagram Drawn 6-19-31
Last Revised 9-30-63

Steel Cabooses of the Chesapeake & Ohio

Chapter 2

Pere Marquette Coach Cabooses

Very little is known about the use of former Pere Marquette passenger coaches in caboose service. Fortunately two photos document that such a situation did exist. The photo below, from the Art Million collection, depicts coach 1100, renumbered to A1100, in local freight service in July 1957. The car was bringing up the markers on the Waverly-to-Muskegon local and was photographed at Grand Haven, Michigan. Crews did not like these caboose conversions and they avoided them if at all possible. Usually a few seats were removed to accommodate a caboose stove and coal bin, and a conductor's desk was installed across the aisle from the stove. Crews complained that the cars were hard to heat in the winter and difficult to get on and off. Pere Marquette coaches 1100-1111 were built in 1921 by Standard Steel Car Company. Series 1200-1209 were converted from Pullman Parlor Cars in 1941. All 10 were sold to Mexico in 1951.

Phil Shuster provided some very interesting additional insight into the use of the A1100-series coaches in caboose service. Phil's comments follow:

"There was a severe caboose shortage throughout the C&O in the mid-1950's. To help alleviate the situation 10 Pere Marquette coaches were converted to cabooses in late 1955 or early 1956. An after-the-fact AFE for $24,000 was approved in July 1957 (AFE 13882) to cover the conversions. It was an interesting contradiction that in this same caboose shortage period 12 wood cabooses were sold to the Toledo Terminal Railroad!

"It was my unfortunate lot to become thoroughly acquainted with the A1102 in August 1956. I was sent up to Walbridge for two weeks to relieve the Assistant Track Supervisor while he went on vacation. The A.T.S's particular responsibility at that time was to supervise the 'Mud Train', a work train operating twice daily between the L.O.F. east Toledo plant, north of Walbridge, and Presque Isle. L.O.F. had a huge settling basin which contained thousands of yards of waste glass sand and particle which they wanted to relocate and the C&O needed fill material at Presque Isle to enable expansion of the yard. We rounded up, purchased, and leased every air dump car we could find available until we had over 40 cars divided into two groups. While L.O.F. loaded one group, the other would be taken by work train over the Toledo Terminal Railroad to Presque Isle and unloaded, hopefully before noon. The empties were returned to L.O.F. and placed for loading that afternoon while the cars loaded that morning were taken to Presque Isle on the second run of the day and unloaded. This operation began early in the spring of 1956 and continued into freezing weather in late autumn. The work train was a bid job so the same crew was on hand each day, and good old A1102 was the assigned caboose.

"The tracks used for both loading and unloading were continually shifted as the work progressed and as a result were uneven and frequently covered with mud spills. That coach would derail at the slightest provocation, and we spent as much time rerailing it as moving mud. As stated previously, the crews hated the old gal. The conductors would continually hound the yardmasters and several times conned them out of a regular caboose if one was available because of vacations, etc.

"Around Walbridge, the A1102 was never used except as a last resort. In the summer of 1959, these 10 coach 'cabooses' were burned at Saginaw and then were cut up for scrap."

The photo of **A1102** (above) was taken in January 1958, at Ottawa Yard, Erie, Michigan. Reportedly this car was used very little and sat in storage at the yard for quite some time. Note the caboose-style curved grab irons by the steps and the safety rails applied across the vestibule opening. There also is an air line with backup whistle. *Kirk Hise*

Once removed from caboose service, the Pere Marquette coach cabooses were accumulated at the PM's Saginaw, Michigan, shops where they were whitelined, then lined up for scrapping. Phil Shuster was on hand to record these two views of the cars at Saginaw in July 1959. Above, the A1111 is shown still on trucks, while the A1103, below, has been set on the ground to await its fate.

14 Steel Cabooses of the Chesapeake & Ohio

Chapter 3

Pere Marquette A901 Series

The first Pere Marquette Railway steel cabooses came on line in 1937 with the delivery of 25 cars from Magor Car Corporation of Passaic, New Jersey. The basic caboose design, developed by the Advisory Mechanical Committee (see chapter 6), was almost identical to C&O's first lot of steel cabooses.

A comparison of PM and C&O early steel cabooses is shown by this table.

ITEM	C&O 90000	PM A901
Weight	42,000 lbs.	42,200 lbs.
Journals	4-1/4" x 8"	5" x 9"
Underframe	Duryea	Steel
Truck Centers	19' 5"	19' 8-1/8"

The first C&O steel-sheathed cabooses were built in July and August 1937, by Magor Car Corporation. This same builder was given the order for the first PM steel-sheathed cabooses and Magor Car outshopped the first PM car less than one month after the last car of the C&O batch had been completed.

Only subtle differences separated the two groups of cars.

C&O's first steel cars used the much-heralded "Duryea" underframe, while the PM cars were built with standard steel underframes. The PM cars rode on secondhand trucks from old PM 81000-series 40-ton box cars, hence their 5 by 9 journals were larger than the 4-1/4 by 8 journals that the C&O 90000-series cars were originally fitted with when new.

Most cars were relettered C&O at either the Wyoming (Grand Rapids) or Saginaw, Michigan, carshops in the late 1940s or early 1950s. During this same time, brakes were changed to "AB" standard.

Although most of the early C&O steel cabooses were rebuilt and renumbered into the 3500 and 3600 series, the PM cabooses received very little modification over the five decades that they were in service. After the mid-1970s the ranks of the A901 series cars quickly thinned. As of late 1984 only two cars were left in active service from the original lot of 25. One of those two remaining cars, 900907, was bad-ordered at Parsons Yard, Columbus, Ohio, on December 10, 1984. Its active days were over. C&O 900920 was the last car of the class left in active service, biding its final time in yard service at Detroit, until being sent to the Grand Rapids shops on Septem-

Secondhand freight car trucks are very evident in the Magor Car Corporation builder's photo of the first PM steel caboose. Notice that the month has yet to be applied to side stencil dates (STD). *C&OHS Collection*

ber 25, 1986, and was put into "Dismantle" category. Fortunately, at least half a dozen cars from this original lot of PM steel cabooses have been preserved by private individuals and organizations.

Photos indicate that the A901-series cabooses never had the typical C&O window awnings over the side windows.

PERE MARQUETTE

Dating back to the earliest wood cabooses, Pere Marquette used the letter "A" as a prefix to the caboose number. Although the reason for this has most likely been lost in the annals of time, general speculation is that it stood for "Accommodation" which indicated a car for the accommodations of the rear crew.

A builder's photo documents the as-built appearance of end appliances. Lettering in 4" characters was applied above the door. (STD) *C&OHS Collection*

"Chesapeake & Ohio" lettering replaced the original Pere Marquette lettering after emergence from the Wyoming paint shop in May 1949. Grand Haven, Michigan, was the location where this April 28, 1950, photo was made. Note that this car wears black markers. (STD) *John C. LaRue Collection*

C&O A917, photographed at Toledo, Ohio, in April 1962, exhibits the revised paint scheme which included application of the first generation "for Progress" emblem. Even though the railroad had adopted the yellow color for cabooses several years earlier, cars did not receive the new scheme until they needed repainting, resulted in red cabooses lasting well into the 1960s. Note that this car is wearing yellow markers. (STD) *Kirk Hise*

16   Steel Cabooses of the Chesapeake & Ohio

The standard C&O yellow scheme, adopted in 1957, is exemplified in this C&O Railway Company view of the A910 taken in November 1964. This photo most likely was taken in Michigan. The car carries a 1962 stencil from Plymouth, and a 1964 date from Flint. (STD)

Caboose A901 and GP 9 6075 are shown on a transfer run to Penn Central's Stanley Yard in Toledo in November 1970. Note the hinged screen applied to the window nearest the smokestack. This type of application was found on many older steel cabooses. Although this car is in relatively fresh paint, the red frame stripe is difficult to discern and may not have been applied. Refer to the painting chapter for more information on red stripes. *Kirk Hise*

Assigned to Columbus, C922, photographed on a transfer run to the N&W in August 1980, displays full running boards and safety appliances. The PM A901-series cabooses originally were delivered with wood running boards, which later were replaced by these steel types. Renumbering cabs to have "C" prefix numbers was a short-lived effort to convert C&O cars to the longtime B&O caboose numbering system. *Dwight Jones*

17

Another caboose assigned to Columbus is the 900907, which had the distinction of being the oldest PM caboose in active service when this photo was taken in December 1984. Previously in the "Walbridge scheme", the smaller-than-normal C&O emblem was reapplied at the request of the author for display at the 1984 C&OHS conference held at Columbus. This view offers a good look at the metal grating on the end platform (which replaced the original wood platforms), and also documents the removal of the running boards, roof safety appliances, and top rung of the ladders. (NON-STD) *Dwight Jones*

(Left) Comparison of this July 1984 end view of 900922 taken at Dayton, Ohio, with the builder's photo that appeared earlier reveals many of the changes made to these cabooses over their nearly five decades of service. Modifications that are readily apparent include metal running boards, a window added to the door, swivel marker reflectors, splash guards, elimination of platform uncoupling chain, and addition of a roof-mounted bracket for the platform angle cock handle. *Dwight Jones*

The Grand Rapids shops had to "wing it" when they applied full Chessie System livery to A920 in 1977. The reason: The Mechanical Department did not prepare an official Chessie lettering diagram for some older steel cabooses until 1981—nearly a decade after introduction of the Chessie image! This photo was taken at Plymouth, Michigan, on May 22, 1980. *Dennis Schmidt*

Cabooses and other non-revenue cars retired after 1982 that had not received a new six-digit road number sometimes had "9s" added as prefixes to their base number to make them six digits. That procedure replaced the previous practice of whitelining the car number and stenciling a "Z" on the sides of cars that had been retired. Photographed at Russell, November 24, 1983. Note the underbody battery box, a rarity on cars from this series. *Dwight Jones*

18   Steel Cabooses of the Chesapeake & Ohio

This photo shows a rather unusual lettering scheme applied to caboose A909 on the North Local at Muskegon, Michigan, around 1949. The cab appears to have the smaller 7" size lettering but without the double donut C&O emblem. Given the car's assignment, one would have expected it to have been painted at Grand Rapids. *Bob Vandevusse / Art Million Collections*

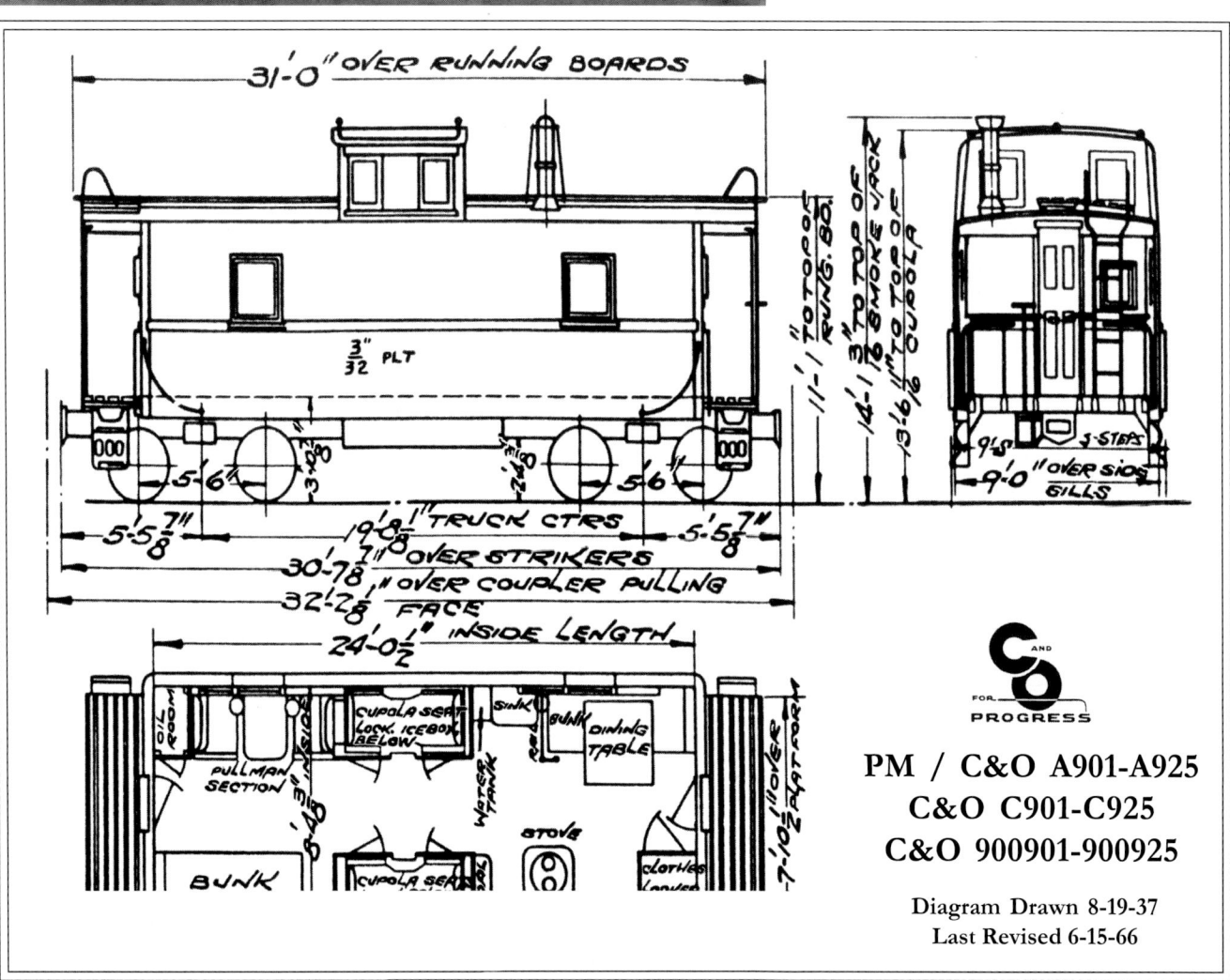

PM / C&O A901-A925
C&O C901-C925
C&O 900901-900925

Diagram Drawn 8-19-37
Last Revised 6-15-66

Chapter 4

Pere Marquette A950 Series

Pere Marquette received its second (and last) group of steel-bodied cabooses in 1941. The St. Louis Car Company assembled 40 cars at its St. Louis, Missouri, facility between September and December 1941. These cars were, for all practical purposes, similar to the PM's first lot of steel-bodied cabs. There were minor dimensional differences, as a comparison of the two diagram sheets shows.

External improvements were more noticeable than the minor dimensional variances. Apex Tri-Lok metal running boards replaced the wooden running boards found on the earlier PM steel cabs. The new A950-series cars also came equipped with new Bettendorf swing-motion trucks—undoubtedly an improvement over the secondhand box car trucks fitted to the Pere Marquette A901-series cars.

The most noticeable external difference was the location of the end ladders. They were moved to the opposite side of the ends from the earlier PM lot[2].

The first car of the series, A950, was specially fitted with a "rod arm arrangement" and "cutout cock" that allowed trainmen standing on the rear platform to turn the air line angle cock from the safety of the end platform. The work was done at the Wyoming (Grand Rapids) car shops and the price was included in the original lot cost for the series. Retrofitting occurred on other cabooses at a later date and likely was also completed at Wyoming or Saginaw.

Historians and modelers are indeed fortunate that the C&O Mechanical Department had the foresight to preserve high-quality builder's photos such as this one of PM caboose A954. Yellow safety appliances made their debut on these PM A950-series cars. (STD) *C&OHS Collection*

20   Steel Cabooses of the Chesapeake & Ohio

Rail historians many times neglect to shoot end or other specialized views of equipment in favor of the classic three-quarter or broadside roster perspective. Other angles are important, too, as shown by this end view of **A954**. A backup whistle shows between the door and the end window. Note lack of door windows. (STD) *C&OHS Collection*

Pere Marquette caboose A957, being used on train #145, is shown in this odd position at Baldwin, Michigan, circa 1953/1954. The car was rebuilt and returned to service but with some significant modifications (see the updated photo on page 24). A kerosene marker still hangs on the caboose. The woman at left exhibits a disgusted look at the whole situation. *Art Million Collection/PM Historical Society Collection*

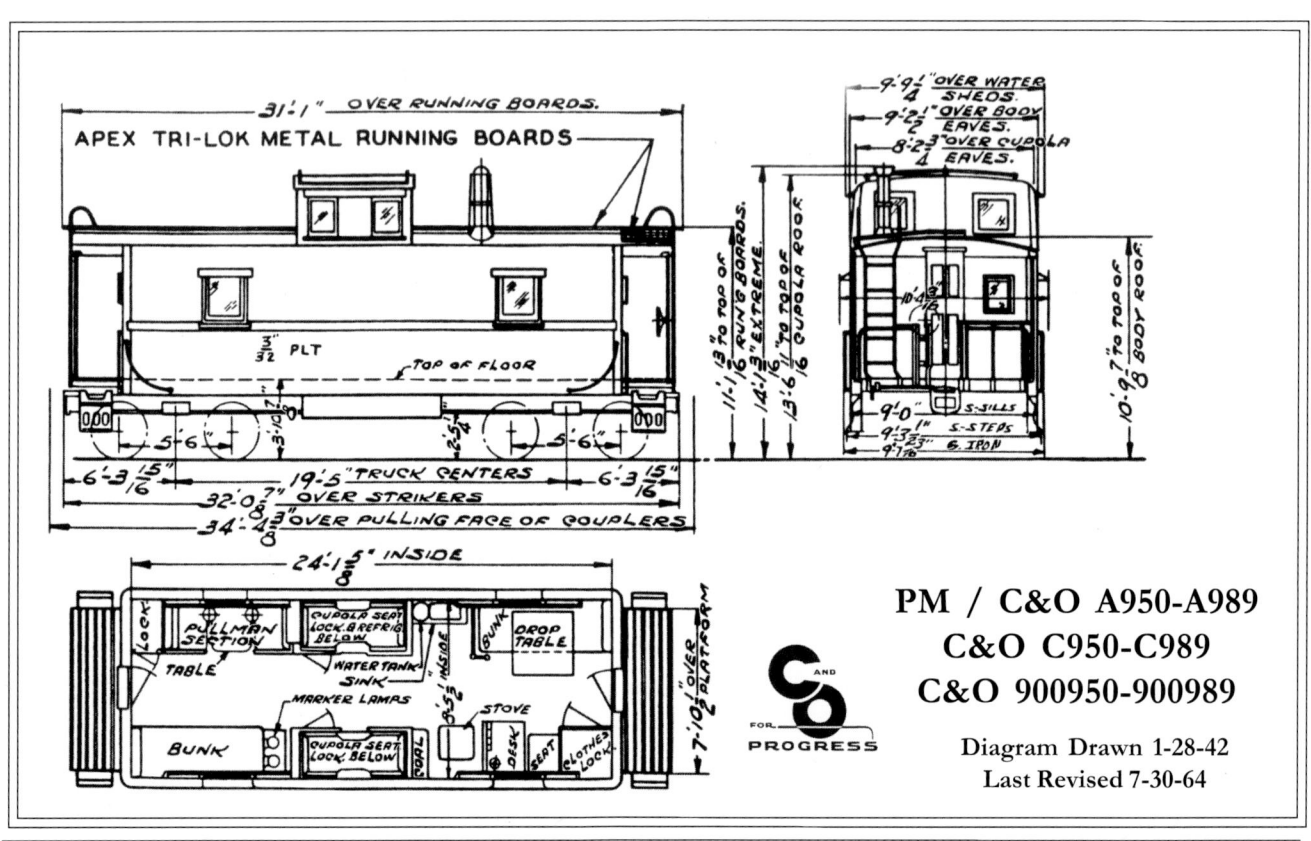

PM / C&O A950-A989
C&O C950-C989
C&O 900950-900989

Diagram Drawn 1-28-42
Last Revised 7-30-64

Steel Cabooses of the Chesapeake & Ohio

Caboose A950 was photographed on the cab track at Detroit on July 9, 1964. It appears to have been painted yellow about two years earlier. This view provides a good look at the splash guards which have been added to the end railings. Note how the side windows slide horizontally. **(STD)** *Eugene A. Ellis*

There were only six cars in the A950 series that received "C" prefixes to their numbers, replacing the Pere Marquette "A". It was an attempt at system consistency for caboose numbers. B&O cabooses had carried "C" prefix numbers since 1908. As it turned out, it was a short-lived program, superseded by another system renumbering that would give cabooses six digit numbers that began with "90", on C&O, B&O and Western Maryland. The C-979 is shown at Columbus on October 21, 1979. Note the heavy repair panels on the side, the addition of swivel reflector markers, and the lack of an "A" applied to the cupola ends when the car was last painted. Perhaps the painters had a premonition of the future renumbering? *Dwight Jones*

Certain cabooses were given both backup lights and FRA marker lights mounted in a metal box installed on the end of the roof. Others, such as A977, photographed at Flint, Michigan, on October 9, 1982, received only the backup light. Most cabooses, though, received only the FRA light. Backup lights were only intended for certain local and mine runs that had to reverse direction with the caboose in the lead. The underframe battery box is an indication that this car has been electrified. Few of the former PM cabs received that extensive treatment. *Dwight Jones*

(Right) An aerial view of a fire-gutted A958 at Columbus, Ohio, in July 1982, provides a look at roof and end platform details. *Dwight Jones*

End view of A957 (with sister C988) on display at the Barbour County, West Virginia, Fairgrounds in September 1984. But, wait a minute...there's something odd about the A957—the ladder is on the wrong side! We spent quite some time inspecting this car in 1984 and finally concluded it had been rebuilt—probably due to a wreck (see page 22). Other subtle differences to the end railings are also visible. See endnote 2 for more ladder information. *Dwight Jones*

Cab A962 is shown whitelined at the Grand Rapids shops on May 28, 1983. It was sold for scrap eight months later to scrap dealer Mansbach Metal of Ashland, Kentucky. It is easy to see how a caboose in this condition could be rebuilt with its ladder moved to the opposite side as displayed on A957 above left. Note how the side windows slide open. End platforms were still wood on this car, but had been converted to steel grating on the A958 shown in the above aerial view. *Dwight Jones*

Chapter 5

Troop Sleeper Cabooses

Troop sleepers have long fascinated both railfans and modelers. This fascination is probably caused in part by the cars' military history and in part by the unique design of the carbody.

Built by Pullman-Standard Car Manufacturing Company for the Defense Plant Corporation, troop sleepers were built for efficiency in transporting military personnel while striving at the same time for some semblance of passenger comfort. They were, in fact, billed as the first cars ever built exclusively for carrying troops.

Based on the standard A.A.R. 50'6" box car design, the cars were of all-steel construction with heavily reinforced ends. They were fully interchangeable with regular passenger equipment, and were equipped with steam train lines and high-speed passenger train car trucks. The trucks were designed especially for the troop cars and became known as the "Allied Full Cushion" truck (see the chapter on trucks).

Each car was equipped for handling 29 military personnel and one Pullman porter. For sleeping purposes, each car was equipped with ten tiers of three berths, offering individual sleeping accommodations for each person. For daytime use the top berth stored bedding and linen supplies. The middle berth was hinged and could be lowered to form the back of a three-passenger seat using the bottom berth as the seat bottom.

The troop sleepers had provisions for thorough ventilation. In addition to standard windows that could be raised and lowered, each car was equipped with eight exhaust ventilators in the roof and inlet ventilators located in the sides near the eaves.

Sanitary facilities were a fundamental necessity. Two washstands and one toilet compartment were located at each end of the cars. Drinking water and disposable cups were also at those locations. The interiors of the cars were finished in

Wearing its new six-digit road number, 911014, formerly X1074, ex-caboose 90457, was photographed outside the Huntington car shops on November 6, 1982. Note that one of the Allied Full Cushion trucks has been replaced by a standard freight car truck. *Dwight Jones*

Troop Sleeper Caboose Roster

Caboose Number	ex WAA Number	To Caboose	Date Built	to MofW Number	to MofW Date	Date Retired	Disposition
90457	8195	6-8-48	1945	X1074	12-7-53	6-9-81	Renumbered 911014 at Grand Rapids
90458	?		1945	X1052	8-31-53	8-20-82	Renumbered 911062 at St. Albans
90459	8340	6-4-48	1945	X1077	11-30-53	12-31-82	Renumbered 911261 at Cincinnati
90460			1945	X1086	9-14-53	12-31-82	Renumbered 911259 at Cincinnati
90461	8072	6-11-48	1945	X1065	12-7-53	2-15-80	Sold to Mansbach Metal, Ashland, KY
90475	?		1945	X1038	9-21-53	9- -75	Sold to Mansbach Metal, Ashland, KY
90476	?		1945	X1041	9-30-53	7-22-82	Renumbered 911057 at Newport News
90477	?		1945	X1029	11-6-53	3-4-85	Renumbered 911074 at Russell, KY
90478	?		1945	X1066	10-7-53	2-15-83	Renumbered 911155 at Columbus, OH
90479	?		1945	X1028	10-7-53	3-31-82	Renumbered 911044 at Saginaw, MI
90480	?		1945	X1042	10-30-53	11-3-70	Sold to Mansbach Metal, Ashland, KY
90481	7194	6-1-48	1945	X1222	11-13-53	4- -74	Sold to Mansbach Metal, Ashland, KY
90482	8049	6-1-48	1945	X1060	11-6-53	1-13-69	Destroyed at Raceland car shops
90483	7471	6-2-48	1945	X1032	11-6-53	4-19-82	Renumbered 911048 at Peru, IN
90484	7195	6-3-48	1945	X1026	11-30-53	9- -75	Sold to Mansbach Metal, Ashland, KY

three-tone tans.

In addition to troop sleeper cars, troop kitchen cars also were built. The kitchen cars, constructed by American Car & Foundry, used the same basic carbody design with necessary interior changes and smaller exterior windows.

Troop sleepers originally were numbered in series 7000-8199, 8300-8499, and 9000-9999, and were built between December 1943 and May 1946 by Pullman. Troop kitchen cars originally were numbered K100-K499 (built September-December 1943) and K504-K550 and K900-K999 (built 1945-1946), and were outshopped by AC&F.[3]

The troop car fleet was operated and maintained by the Pullman Company, which took its responsibility seriously. The cars served America well, and after the war were declared surplus by the government. The War Assets Administration (WAA)[4] was given the responsibility of disposing of the fleet. The cars were sold, many through equipment brokers, to railroads that used the former troop cars in a multitude of different services. Cars acquired by C&O and Pere Marquette, for instance, eventually saw service as baggage cars, express cars, camp cars, yard offices, a steam generator car, a station, and, oh yes, caboose cars.

In 1948 15 troop sleepers were outfitted for caboose service on the C&O (probably at the Raceland car shops). A diagram was prepared by C&O's Mechanical Department for these cars, but unfortunately no photos have turned up showing the cars in actual caboose service. The caboose troop sleepers were numbered in series 90457-90461 and 90475-90484. Their

C&O camp car X1041 was photographed at Windsor Shades, Virginia, on February 28, 1975. This car was renumbered to 911057 at Newport News on July 22, 1982. It originally was C&O caboose 90476. *Charles H. Cox*

use as cabooses was relatively short-lived, and all were renumbered to "X" series camp cars in 1953 (apparently at Peru, Indiana). The receipt of 150 new cabooses in 1949 likely eliminated the need for these makeshift cabooses. Nine of the original 15 caboose troop sleepers and 119 of the other 237 C&O troop cars were left in maintenance of way service in late 1985.

Realizing the importance and historical significance of the troop sleeper, C&O prepared to preserve a car for future generations at the B&O Railroad Museum in Baltimore. Car X1183 was selected for the honor and was accordingly removed from the roster in 1976. Unfortunately, the car never reached the museum.[5]

Why not? Jerry Ballard wrote to us after publication of the first edition of this book to advise that this same X1183 was delivered by the C&O to the Hocking Valley Scenic Railway around 1976. No one on the HVSR knew anything about this car and so notified the C&O. After about a week the switcher from Columbus picked up the car and returned it to Columbus. Thereafter it was believed to be scrapped. There was no record of the car ever being renumbered to the six-digit MofW numbers of the 1980s.

For an eyewitness account of C&O caboose troop sleepers refer to end note 6.

An end view shows former caboose 90459 at Columbus on October 6, 1984. One spotting feature for troop sleepers used as cabooses is the small diagonal grabiron just under the road number. Diagram sheets indicate this handhold was applied only to caboose troop sleepers. Of the nine remaining troop sleeper cabooses (in 1987), seven had the unique handhold and two did not. In addition, one car was discovered that had the handhold and was not listed as a former caboose—X1083. This could possibly indicate that numbers were inadvertently switched on at least two cars. *Dwight Jones*

A broadside view shows former caboose troop sleeper 90459 at Columbus, Ohio, on October 6, 1984. The car is painted green, roof aluminum, trucks black, grabirons yellow, underbody tank aluminum. The old number was painted over with black paint, and the new number was applied in white. The C&O reporting marks are in yellow. *Dwight Jones*

Caboose 90457, as X1029, was used for a period as a temporary station at Bremo, Virginia, replacing the original depot which was destroyed in a flood of the James River in 1972. The flood also took out highway bridges and the Buckingham Subdivision bridge. This photograph was taken on December 22, 1973. The car was still at this location when photographed by the author on July 30, 1983 and again in August 1986. It later was reported as renumbered at Russell to 911074 on March 4, 1985. *Charles H. Cox*

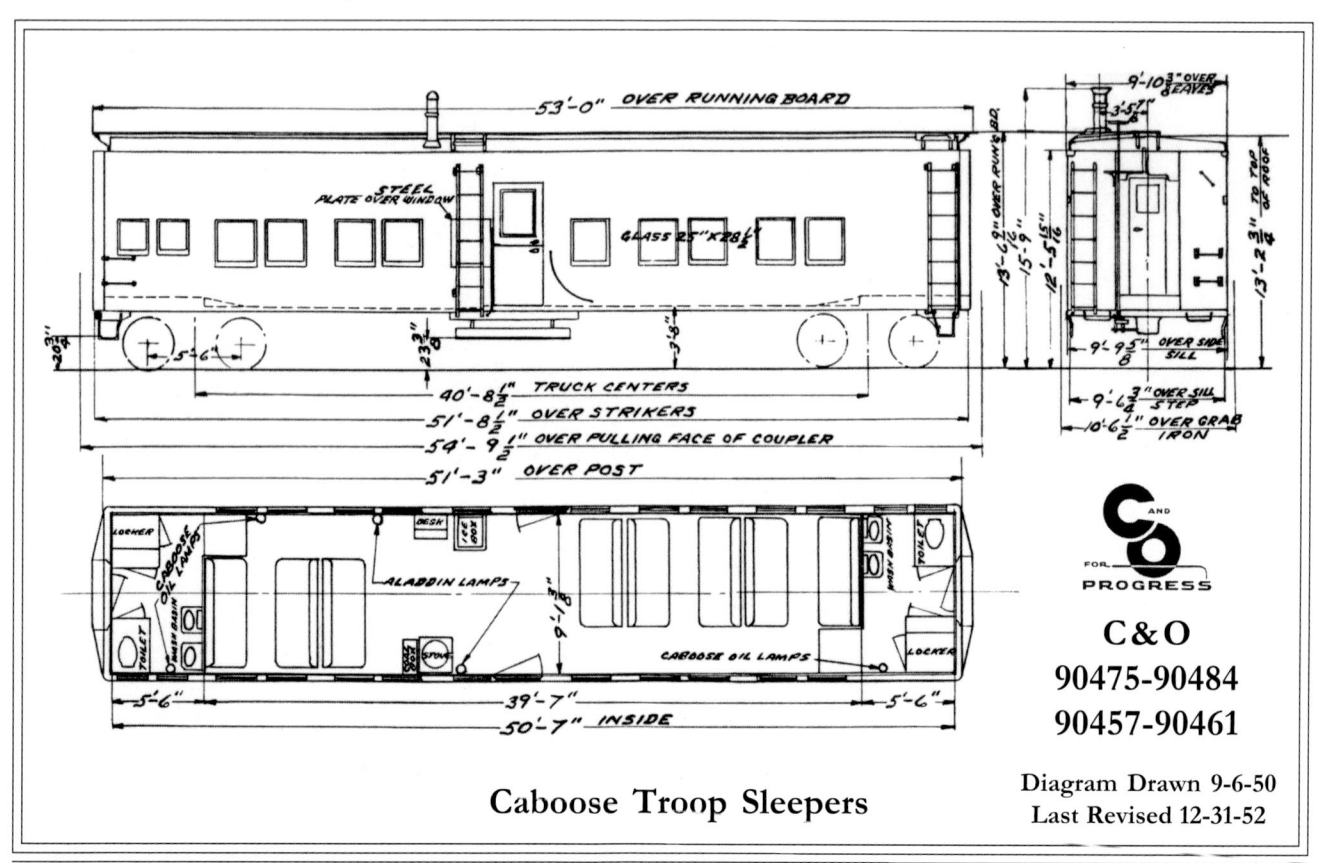

Caboose Troop Sleepers

C&O
90475-90484
90457-90461

Diagram Drawn 9-6-50
Last Revised 12-31-52

28 Steel Cabooses of the Chesapeake & Ohio

Chapter 6

C&O 90000 Series

In 1937 the Chesapeake & Ohio received its first production lot of steel-carbody cabooses.[7] In July and August of that year, the Magor Car Corporation of Passaic, New Jersey, constructed 50 cabooses numbered 90000 to 90049.

It had been nearly a decade since the 1929 delivery of 125 wood-sheathed cabooses from the former Hocking Valley shops at Logan, Ohio. A comparison of those cars, numbered originally 90900 to 91024, with the new steel cars can be seen in the following table.

ITEM	Last Wood Cars	First Steel Cars
Underframe	steel	Duryea
Journals	4-1/4" x 8"	4-1/4" x 8"
Weight	41,500 lbs.	42,000 lbs.
Truck Centers	19' 5"	19' 5"
Inside Length	24' 1/2"	24' 1/2"
Length Over Strikers	30' 6-1/4"	32' 7/8"

Chesapeake & Ohio entered the steel caboose era later than many other class 1 roads. The first steel caboose has been credited to the Pennsylvania Railroad for their 1914-built car. Other major roads such as N&W, B&O, Rock Island, Santa Fe, Reading and Western Maryland (to name just a few), built or acquired their first steel caboose cars during the 1920s and 1930s.

Existing documents indicate that the design for the new C&O steel cabooses was planned and refined by the Advisory Mechanical Committee, headquartered at Cleveland. Among other duties, the A.M.C. had the responsibility for coordinating mechanical department functions of the C&O, Erie Railroad, Nickel Plate Road (NYC & STL), and Pere Marquette Railway Company—all of which were controlled by the Van Sweringen brothers of Cleveland

C&O eventually purchased a total of 350 cabooses (not counting PM cars) of the A.M.C. design. This style of caboose was also used by the Pere Marquette, Missouri Pacific, and the Chicago & Eastern Illinois.

The ranks of the 90000-series cars diminished quickly with the rebuilding of 46 of the 50 cars in 1969 and 1970. Rebuilt cars were numbered into the 3500 and 3600 series. Three of the 50 cars had been retired before the rebuilding program started. That left only one car, 90002, to survive into the late 1970s. Company records indicated it was sold to a private owner in 1980. In early 2010 it finally turned up when we received a call from the current owner of the caboose.

The first new steel caboose for Chesapeake & Ohio emerged from the Magor Car plant in July 1937, as evidenced by the build date stenciled on the car. Official C&O records show an August 1937 build date. Note the lack of side window awnings as built. (STD) *C&OHS Collection*

Summary of Retirements

  3 cars retired 1947-1962
46 cars rebuilt to 3500/3600 series
  1 car sold in 1980 to a private owner
50 cars total

An end view shows the first new C&O steel caboose in 1937. Caboose numbers above the end doors lasted until the 1957 adoption of the yellow scheme, at which time the last digits of the caboose number were moved to the cupola ends. Note that the car initial and number show under the coupler. **(STD)** *C&OHS Collection*

Caboose 90011 was repainted at the Parsons Yard shops at Columbus in April 1948. Prior to that it was shopped in December 1947 at Parsons. Those two shopping dates are an indication this car was assigned out of Columbus. By the time of this Parsons repainting, yellow grabirons had been adopted. The car also wears yellow marker lights. The builder photos of 90000 show the car without window awnings (which C&O called "water sheds"). C&O drawing 139-11-288 was revised 2-18-39 to add them.
Paul Dunn, Dwight Jones Collection

Steel Cabooses of the Chesapeake & Ohio

While the painters at the Peru, Indiana, C&O shops were applying red paint to caboose 90048 in May 1957, Mechanical Department personnel were at work, also, at their headquarters, changing the painting and lettering diagram to call for yellow as the main body color. That change was dated May 15, 1957. Probably 90048 was one of the last C&O cabooses to be painted red. But note that the older monogram was used on this car. This older emblem had been phased out 2-1/2 years earlier.
Paul Dunn, Dwight Jones collection

C&O 90001 is believed to be the first caboose painted into the yellow scheme. For evaluation purposes the lettering was different on each side (see page 123). The car was painted at the Raceland carshops. The scheme on the opposite side was the one actually adopted. As evidenced by this photo, the car returned to service wearing the oddball scheme and likely was photographed at Columbus, Logan or Nelsonville. *Paul Dunn, Dwight Jones Collection*

Some first generation steel cabooses received vents on their sides, as shown on 90017. They are typically associated with the installation of electrical equipment to power radios or lights. Most later were welded over with steel plate. The emblem applied to this car appears smaller than the normal emblem. The red side stripe either was not applied to this caboose, or has faded to be invisible. *Paul Dunn, Dwight Jones collection*

Although the underframes of most early steel cabooses were equipped with racks to carry rerailers, photos indicate they were most often missing. An exception is shown on 90004 at Logan, Ohio, in the 1960s. (STD) *Paul Dunn, Dwight Jones collection*

31

Diagram Drawn 7-29-37
Last Revised 5-29-70

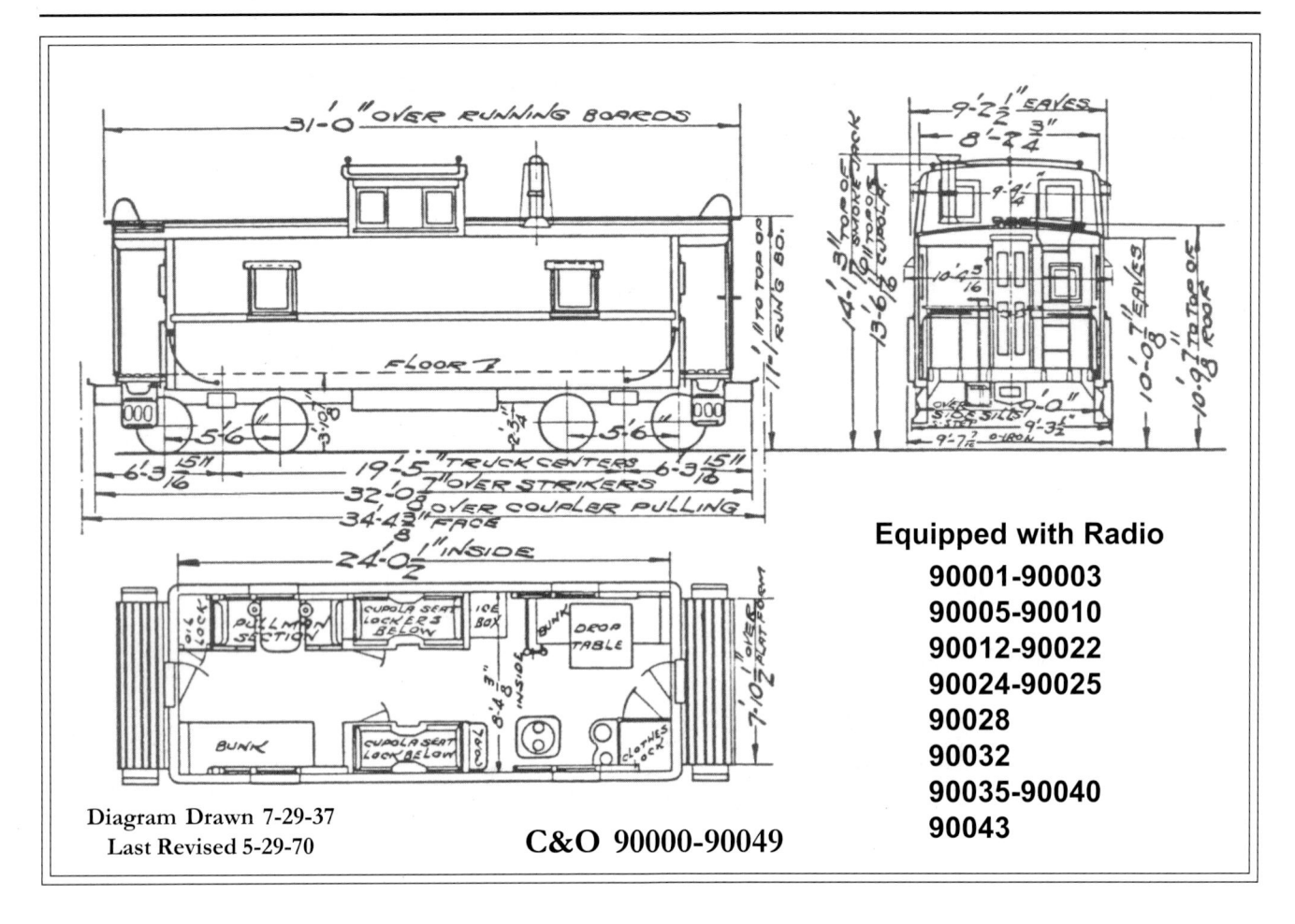

C&O 90000-90049

Equipped with Radio
90001-90003
90005-90010
90012-90022
90024-90025
90028
90032
90035-90040
90043

Railroad Radio Evolution

Those readers accustomed to the widespread use of radio by railroads in the 21st Century may have difficulty understanding railroad operation without radio as it was before the 1950s. Before WWII the use of radio in railroad application was, except in the rarest instances, unheard of. World War II introduced the development of smaller, less costly sets which could meet the railroads' needs. Thus by the mid-1950s sets small enough and affordable came on the market (handheld sets for use by crewmen were still years in the future).

Communication between caboose and locomotive was by whistle or horn, flag and hand signals, or by adjustment in the trainline air pressure which could be made from the caboose. A message or communication with lineside operators or the dispatcher required a train to stop so a crew member could use a trackside telephone. To be able to contact the dispatcher, either directly or through an operator, using a radio, seemed like a wonderful miracle.

The biggest problem encountered with the early radio sets was keeping them functioning as intended, partially due to their rough environment. As time moved along, the radios have become totally reliable and function over distances only dreamed of just a few years ago. Wayside telephones are seldom used today and nearly every trainman is equipped with a radio hanging on his or her hip. *Phil Shuster*

These Motorola PT500 radios were the standard caboose radio during the late Chessie System era. One of these could be found mounted in each road caboose, typically in a bracket, maintained by a padlock to prevent theft. The radios even were delivered in Chessie System yellow. A roof-mounted antenna connected to the radio at top left. *Dwight Jones*

Early C&O Radio Cabooses

As can be seen from the diagram sheets in this book, a number of first-generation C&O steel cabooses were equipped with radios, the first large-scale application to cabooses on the railroad. An article appeared in the August 30, 1954, *Railway Age* magazine documenting the use of radios on the C&O. That article has been condensed here.

C&O installed radios in a total of 38 cabooses along with 71 locomotives (diesel "A" cab units) and in six wayside stations between Columbus and Toledo, a distance of 120 miles. The specific numbers for the cabooses is shown on diagram sheets and provides insight into the actual cabooses operating between Columbus and Toledo. The Division Superintendent also had a radio installed in his car for talking with train crews and monitoring communications.

Other roads crossed the C&O at six interlockings on this line. Heavy coal and ore trains took their chances at getting a proceed signal at these points. With the use of radios, when trains were within eight miles of the crossing they could radio the tower operator and either be told to continue at normal speed, or to reduce speed due to the interlocking being occupied by another road. This helped to reduce the need for these heavy trains to stop and restart.

During 1953 there were an average of 12 daily trains (each way) on this line, with peak activity around 30 trains. In addition to coal and ore, one passenger train operated on the line in each direction, as did extra trains, described as fruit trains with citrus fruit from Florida and apples and peaches from the Carolinas and Georgia.

Benefits of the radio installations were listed as:
1. dispatcher can efficiently plan movements
2. trains don't block highway crossings
3. train inspection information is relayed to interested parties
4. reduced delays in the case of train emergency stops
5. verbal orders allow for efficient train departures from yards
6. everyone is kept informed concerning operations

In the caboose, the radio was installed under one of the cupola seats, with the controls, handset and loudspeaker on the cupola wall. The caboose had a 12-volt DC power supply system which operated from a Leece-Neville generator driven off an axle. That application charged a storage battery to supply a vibrator-converter. The battery, charging equipment and vibrator-converter were located under a seat bunk at one end of the caboose. An air vent, in the caboose side wall, provided ventilation for the battery.

The radio station at Columbus was located in the Dispatcher's Office. To contact a train, the dispatcher used the existing lineside phone system to call the nearest wayside station, requesting that station call the train by radio and then plug the radio into the lineside phone system so the Dispatcher could talk directly with the train crew.

All end-to-end and train-to-train radio calls were made on channel 1 (160.41). For calls between wayside offices, channel 2 (161.31) was used. To obtain semi-privacy, single-channel receivers and dual-channel transmitters were used. Wayside office receivers picked up calls only on channel 2, while receivers on trains picked up only channel 1. Thus wayside operators normally could not hear calls between trains, or between engineers and conductors on the same train. Likewise, train crews could not hear calls between wayside operators. When the wayside operator desired to call a train, the operator would switch over to channel 1. When the engineer or the conductor desired to call a wayside operator, they would switch over to channel 2 and make the call.

To call the dispatcher in an emergency, the conductor would switch over to channel 2, and depress the "dispatcher key" for a few seconds. This operation transmitted a tone which served to connect the radio equipment at the nearest wayside station to the dispatcher's telephone line.

The C&O's communication department at Richmond compiled a monthly analysis of radio troubles. These monthly records revealed recurring failures which often could be eliminated by changes in techniques or servicing, or by modification of existing equipment. The monthly trouble chart also revealed the service life of the units. The average service life for receivers checked during a two month period was 2.1 months, and the average transmitter life was found to be 3.6 months. Analysis showed, for example, that the major weakness in the equipment was tube failure.

The radio project was planned and installed by the C&O's assistant superintendent of communications with radio equipment from Westinghouse Electric Corporation.

The conductor uses a caboose radio to give his engineer a verbal highball. Note speaker mounted to cupola wall.

The map at right shows the C&O line between Columbus and Toledo and identifies the location of the wayside radio stations. This line generally is level with grade and curvature so slight that they do not appreciably affect train speeds. Maximum authorized speed was 75 mph for passenger trains and 50 mph for freight trains. The railroad was double track at the time with center sidings. The two main tracks were signaled for right-hand running, except for 20 miles between Delaware and Marion, where each track was signaled for either direction running. The dispatcher, by means of centralized traffic control, could operate signals and switches at the ends of sidings and some main-track crossovers. He had a control machine with a track diagram indicating locations of trains on main tracks.

Nine Offices Could Call Trains

Crews of moving trains could talk via radio to nine different C&O wayside offices: (1) Columbus dispatcher's office, (2) Parsons yard, (3) Delaware, (4) MA Cabin, Marion, (5) MD Cabin, Marion, (6) Upper Sandusky, (7) Fostoria, (8) Pemberville, and (9) VR Tower, Walbridge yard.

More on C&O Radio Cabooses

The previous information in this chapter was prepared mostly from an article in *Railway Age*. Additional information, presented below, on early C&O radio cabooses was obtained from old Transportation Department caboose files.

Radios were being installed in C&O steel cabooses at least as early as 1953. AFE 20856 was temporarily deferred in January 1953, but was approved by management in March and provided approval to equip 31 cabooses on the Hocking Division with radios. The work was to be assigned to the car shops at Russell, Kentucky. Work on the first caboose was to begin on or around April 13.

C&O correspondence indicated that caboose 90013 was received at Columbus on May 21, 1953, after receiving a radio at Russell. Cab 90102 was sent from Columbus to Russell on May 23, 1953; cab 90014 was sent from Columbus to Russell on May 25, and 90106 was sent to Russell for radio installation from Columbus on June 7. On June 9 officials at the Russell shops instructed officers at Columbus not to send any additional cabooses to Russell for radio installation because it had been found that the blueprints for

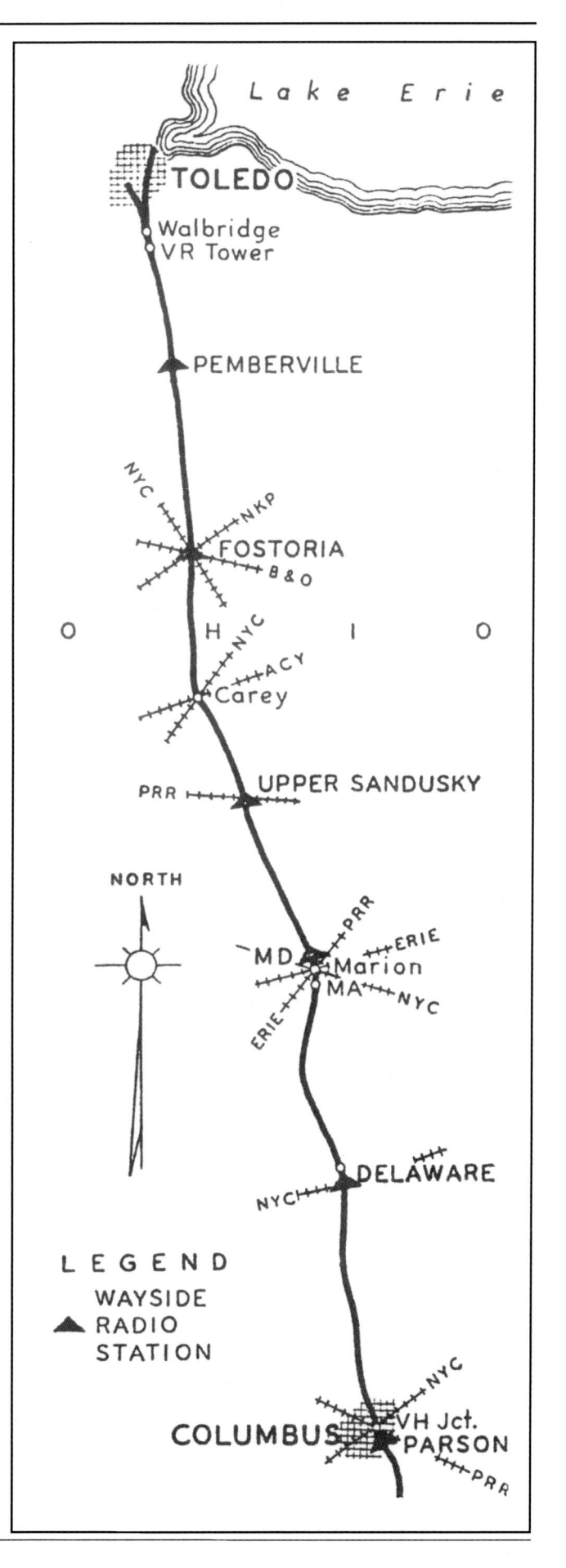

34   Steel Cabooses of the Chesapeake & Ohio

these installations were not correct and needed revision before future work could be completed. It would seem logical to conclude that these may have been the first cabooses equipped with radios based on the drawing errors discovered during installation work on these four cars at Russell.

Caboose 90001 was pictured twice in the book and was shown wearing two different early yellow paint schemes. This was the first C&O caboose painted into the yellow scheme. Company records indicate that a radio was installed in this particular caboose at Russell on January 29, 1954. The large vents installed in the sides of this car for ventilation purposes for the heavy duty diesel radio generator are very visible in the photo of cab 90001 that appears on page 123.

Phil Shuster provides interesting additional information from his days of C&O employment:

"Another of my work assignments during late June and most of July 1956 was supervising a Speno Ballast cleaner work train on the mainline between Columbus and Walbridge. This was a bid job for the train crew and was attractive and much sought after because of the expected overtime. The bid was awarded to the top seniority conductor on the Hocking Division, one Walter Davis. Walter brought along with him his caboose, the 90001, also the first yellow caboose on the railroad. I can confirm that this caboose was lettered differently on opposite sides. That's the way it was at the 1956 Stockholderama and that's the way she stayed in service until her next painting [90001 was reported repainted in 1964 and again 12-10-67-dj].

"This caboose was radio equipped and electricity for the radio was derived from a motor-driven generator housed in a closet in the corner of the cabin. The vents in the side, visible next to the people on the stairway in the photo on page 123, provided air for this motor-generator. It doesn't show in either photo but I believe I remember a small exhaust vent in the roof near the cupola. The fuel tank is visible just ahead of the rear truck.

"The motor-generator equipped cabooses were purposely designed for slow moving work trains where radio use was virtually constant (we fouled the adjacent main and had to retract the machinery to allow trains to pass—all handled via radio). No way that an axle-generator would keep batteries charged on a work train moving one mile per hour for ten hours per day."

Steel Cabooses Originally Assigned to the Hocking Division

Effective 8-22-66
Paint Data Updated to Late 1967

Cab #	Date Painted	Comments
90001	12-10-67	diesel engine equipped for radio power
90002	1964	
90003	2-1-66	
90004	1964	
90005	7-20-66	
90006	1965	
90007	3-9-66	
90008	5-15-66	
90009	3-30-66	
90010	3-8-67	
90012	1-6-66	
90013	1-4-66	
90014	1-26-66	
90015	4-4-66	
90016	5-12-66	
90017	2-19-66	
90018		sent to Peru, IN, 12-26-63
90019	2-28-65	
90020	9-17-66	(also reported as painted 9-12-65)
90021	2-24-66	
90022		destroyed in derailment 3-20-62
90023		sent to Peru, IN, 12-23-56
90024	3-14-66	
90025	11-25-66	
90102		
90103		sent to Walbridge, OH, 12-23-64
90105	3-14-66	
90106	4-14-66	
90107		diesel engine equipped for radio power
90231	2-4-66	
90232		diesel engine equipped for radio power
90233		diesel engine equipped for radio power
90234	11-5-66	
90235	12-5-66	
90236		diesel engine equipped for radio power
90237	6-12-66	diesel engine equipped for radio power
90238	1-7-67	
90261	8-5-66	diesel engine equipped for radio power

90232 was reported as sent to Peru, IN, 2-6-56.
90236 was reported as sent to Walbridge, OH, 2-15-62.

Chapter 7

C&O 90050 Series

Between 1941 and 1947 the C&O added 150 steel cabooses to its fleet. These new cars were obtained in three lots, and from three different caboose builders. Built to the same General Arrangement drawing as C&O's earlier group of 50 steel cabooses, these 150 cars differed mostly in car builder and air brake manufacturer.

SERIES	BUILDER	AIR BRAKE Manufacturer
90050-90099	Magor Car	Westinghouse
90100-90149	St. Louis Car	New York Air
90150-90199	AC&F	Westinghouse

In January 1966 specifications were changed to upgrade the interiors of all cabooses in the 90000-90349 series. See chapter 9 for a description of those changes.

Retirements started in 1945, when two cars were retired on the same date at the Russell carshops. Four additional cars had been retired by the late 1960s.

One car, 90099, was sold in 1967 to B&O to alleviate a very interesting predicament. System-wide caboose pooling was being implemented on the B&O and the road had negotiated with the unions to have 197 cabooses fitted up for this system-wide service. New cabooses were purchased and older cabs upgraded at company shops to conform to the system pool requirements. When all work was completed, B&O was one car short of the agreed-to total of 197. The solution was to purchase one car from the C&O. The C&O car was upgraded and modified at B&O's Du Bois, Pennsylvania, shops, and was given B&O number C-3050 in the B&O caboose numbering system. During the Chessie System era, this was the only steel cupola caboose on the B&O, a road that preferred bay-window cabooses.

In 1969 and 1970, 139 cars from the series were rebuilt at the Grand Rapids car shops and were renumbered to the 3500-3684 series (see chapter 13). Two additional cars were retired in the 1970s, leaving only two cars from the original 150 on the roster by 1984.

SUMMARY OF RETIREMENTS
- 6 cars retired 1945-1953
- 1 car sold to B&O in 1967
- 139 cars rebuilt to 3500-3684 series
- 2 cars retired 1976-1979
- 2 cars retired 1986, 1987

150 Total Cars

American Car & Foundry posed 90193 for builder's photos at its Chicago plant in 1947 to represent series 90150-90199, their contribution to the 150 cars acquired by the C&O. Yellow grabirons were standard attire by this date. This caboose was rebuilt in 1969 to become C&O 3584. (STD) *C&OHS Collection*

Steel Cabooses of the Chesapeake & Ohio

At St. Louis, Missouri, a C&O caboose from series 90100-90149 moves along the St. Louis Car Company assembly line on antique arch bar shop trucks with wood blocking. *C&OHS Collection*

C&O drawing 191-7-39 documented the application of steel grating to end platforms on caboose series 90000-90349 with a drawing date of October 20, 1967.

Sherwin-Williams red paint glistens on the side of 90119 as photographed at the St. Louis Car plant in 1941. Note that safety appliances, including marker light brackets, are painted black. Although the background has been eliminated in this SLC photo, the caboose appears to be in a building with outside light illuminating the end, giving some the incorrect impression that the end is painted a lighter color than the sides of the caboose. (STD) *C&OHS Collection*

Comparison of end views of 90193 (1947) and 90124 (1982) shows some interesting changes. Caboose 90124 has been modified with an Ajax-type brake wheel (note that the car also has been given a vertical post extending to the roof), metal running boards, an end door with window panes added to the upper section, standard C&O-style marker reflectors, and backup light. The missing knuckle in the coupler of 90124 attests to its bad-order status at Flint, Michigan. **(STD) (STD)** *C&OHS Collection (90193) and Dwight Jones (90124)*

37

Caboose 90105 is shown in fresh paint at Athens, Ohio, on November 11, 1949. The car last was painted at the Parsons Yard shops at Columbus in July 1949, using Sherwin-Williams paint. Although painting specs were revised to include the monogram in 1948, it was not applied to this car. *Bob's Photo*

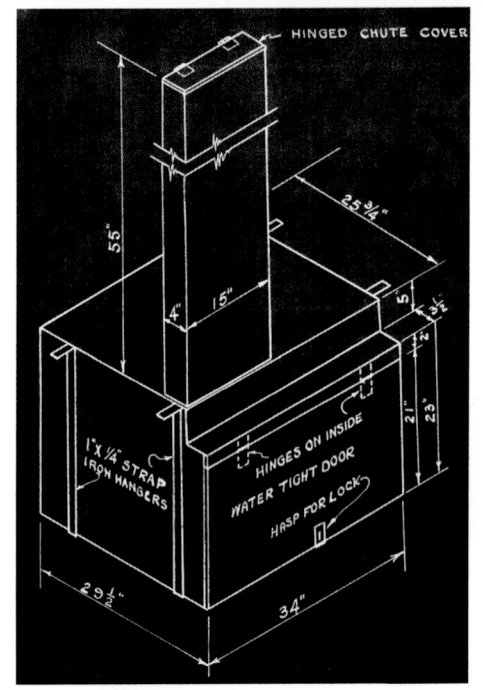

C&O Mail Cabooses

The mystery of C&O mail cabooses began with the discovery of C&O drawing B-176 dated 2-13-48 which depicted an underbody mail compartment with a chute (see drawing at left) and the application of that equipment to a C&O caboose in series 90000-90049 for service at Peru, Indiana. The photo below of caboose 90150 was taken at Peru on June 23, 1949, and appears to show that application in use. A photo of sister Peru caboose 90151 photographed from the opposite side appears to show an application to that car also.

The "chute" on this device extended upward through the floor of the cupola and had a hinged lid. It appears that someone sitting in the cupola seat could deposit mail into the chute and it would feed into the box below.

We have no other information on this fascinating arrangement. But, the date of the drawing and date of the caboose photo is very close to the October 25, 1949 date of the last C&O passenger train to operate through Peru. Did C&O have a mail contract with the U.S. Government which had to continue past the date of the passenger train discontinuance, hence the use of the cabooses? *C&O drawing B-176 from C&OHS archives; photo of 90150 Bob's Photo*

38   Steel Cabooses of the Chesapeake & Ohio

The C&O photographer coaxed this venerable conductor to pose for a portrait at Huntington, West Virginia, in the late 1950s. We wonder if that's the conductor's 1956 Kentucky license plate mounted to the cupola roof. Such unique fixtures were quite common in years past and helped conductors to locate "their" car among long strings of similar-looking cabooses on cab tracks. **(STD)** *C&OHS Collection*

C&O 90160 exhibits hardly any variation over its as-built appearance in this photo, most likely taken in the 1960s. A long extension handle to turn the angle cock from the end platform appears to be the only upgrade. The yellow paint scheme with blue lettering and red side stripe, is applied exactly as the company painting and lettering drawing dictated. **(STD)** *Paul Dunn/Dwight Jones Collection*

The next-to-the-last of the 150 cars in the 90050 series to be carried as active in company records was 90124 (later 900124). The car was photographed at Flint, Michigan, in October 1982. It was stenciled as a "dismantle" in October 1984. Note the underbody battery box, backup light, and small vent in the upper right corner, most likely an indication of an interior toilet compartment. Even with these electric enhancements, the car retains its reflectorized markers. A power brake stand is an upgrade, as is an additional post to the right of the brake wheel. *Dwight Jones*

Over a dozen C&O and former Pere Marquette first-generation steel cabooses are shown at Shelby, Kentucky. It's pure C&O in this August 15, 1970, view. But it would not last. Twenty-four months away were new 4100-series GP40-2 locomotives—they would hail the beginning of the Chessie System era. *T. W. Dixon, Jr.*

Duryea Cushion Underframe

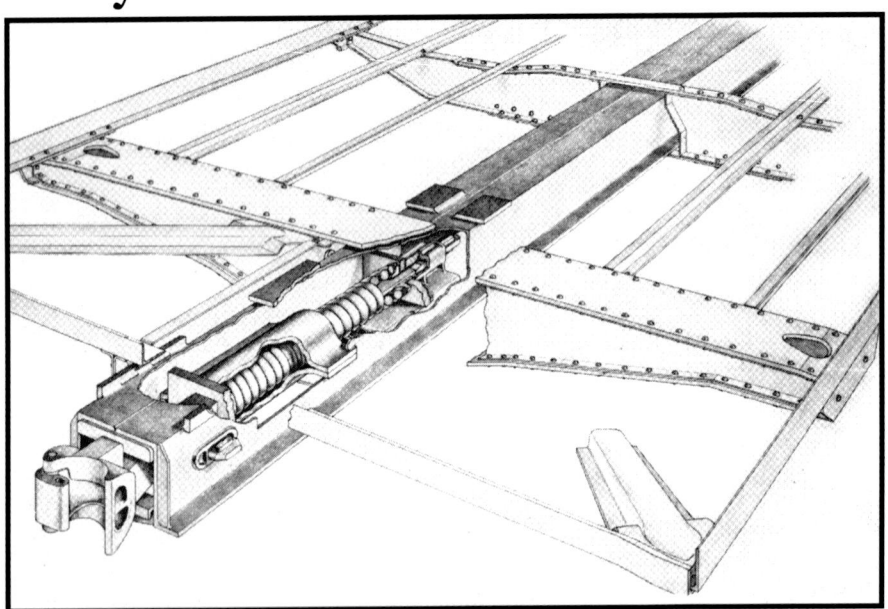

Early C&O steel cabooses (90000-90349, PM A950-series and ex-WM cabs) were equipped with Duryea underframes. This type underframe was advertised as having several advantages including a travel of seven inches over which to distribute stresses due to buff or pull, and yet reduce slack action to a minimum. The cutaway diagram shows the shock absorbing springs of the simplest design. Various other arrangements were offered by the O.C. Duryea Corporation of New York, depending on car type and load limits. The diagram shown here most likely was applied to cabooses. When the C&O rebuilt many of these first-generation cabs to the 3500-3684 series in the late 1960s, the official diagram sheet indicates that the original Duryea underframes were retained. That's not much of a surprise. It would likely have been cost prohibitive to change out that equipment. And there really was no need to retrofit the cars since cabooses were not expected to go off-line to other railroads. The Duryea underframe was banned from interchange service by the AAR effective July 1, 1972.[8]

Photos indicate that a few first generation C&O steel cabooses were modified by having the original end window, located to the right of the door, sealed with a metal plate and a new window added to the left of the door. Such modifications typically indicate an interior alteration such as adding a closet or sanitary compartment in the corner. No information has been discovered to explain this modification, which is shown on the 90100, probably photographed in the late 1960s. *Paul B. Dunn collection*

40 Steel Cabooses of the Chesapeake & Ohio

It's rare to find older roof views of cabooses that show wood running boards, as on 90169 in this photo. Veteran photographer Gene Huddleston caught K-2 1167 in pusher service near Barboursville, West Virginia, in June 1955 with an eastbound coal train. Gene remembers that the K-2 had recently been recalled from long-term storage; it was one of two pushers stationed at St. Albans, West Virginia. The train had originated at Logan, West Virginia.

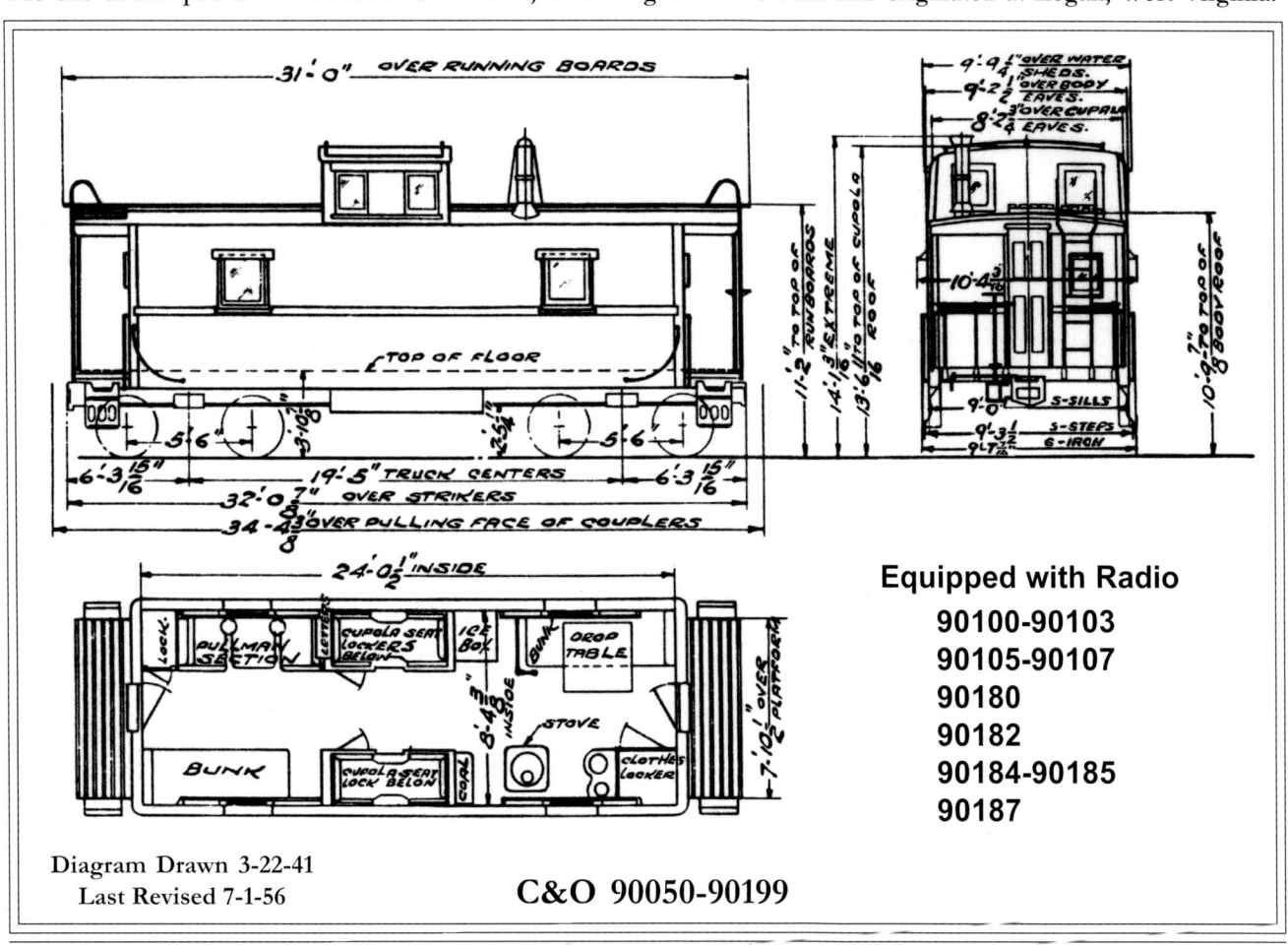

Equipped with Radio
90100-90103
90105-90107
90180
90182
90184-90185
90187

Diagram Drawn 3-22-41
Last Revised 7-1-56

C&O 90050-90199

41

Chapter 8

C&O 90200 Series

As the decade of the 1940s was coming to a close, new cabooses were once again en route to C&O lines. It had only been two and a quarter years since the delivery of cab 90199 in 1947. Now, 150 new cars were being built for C&O by American Car and Foundry—100 cars for the Chesapeake District, numbered 90200-90299, and 50 cars for the Pere Marquette District, numbered 90300-90349.

The Chesapeake District cars were delivered in July and August 1949, and differed from the PM District 90300-series cars primarily in the placement of the end ladders and interior arrangement details. See endnote 2 for more information on C&O's end ladder oddities.

In January 1966, specifications were changed to upgrade interior accommodations of cabooses in the series 90000-90349. See chapter 9 for a description of those changes. No records exist to indicate which cars or how many cars actually received the modifications.

Many cars in the 90200 series were upgraded at the Grand Rapids shops between 1980 and 1982. This upgrading included removal of window awnings, installation of new windows with FRA-approved glass, installation of new end doors, and a new coat of Chessie paint. In addition, most cars received electric lights and underbody battery compartments.

The vast majority of 90200-series cars were still in service in 1984. Only 17 of the original 100 cars had been retired by that date. The first car to be removed from the series left the roster in 1959, when 90284 was destroyed at the Raceland car shops.

Most of the cars that remained in service in the 1980s were assigned to the West Virginia and Kentucky coalfields for use on mine runs out of such locations as Peach Creek, Shelby, Paintsville, Danville, and Elk Run Junction. Additional cars were assigned to major terminals such as Cincinnati and Toledo for use in yard puller service. It is these terminal cabs that, in general, were not equipped with electric marker lights and underbody battery boxes.

The last car from the series, 900219, was donated by CSX to the C&O Historical Society and today can be found in fully restored condition (in red paint) at Clifton Forge, Virginia.[9]

Last of the Chesapeake District cars, 90299, posed for a builder's portrait in August 1949. The car exhibits the current caboose lettering scheme featuring the first generation "for Progress" emblem. Small lettering above the left truck proclaims that the car is equipped with a "Duryea Cushion Underframe", a big deal at the time. The new cabooses came with power brake stands on each end, but retained wood end platforms. (STD) *C&OHS collection*

Caboose 90296 was only five months old when the C&O photographer snapped this photo at Russell, Kentucky, in January 1950. The conductor of an eastbound is about to grab the flimsies (train orders) from the operator at RU Cabin. Thirty-six years later, in 1986, cabooses were being eliminated in favor of end-of-train devices with the conductor then riding the head end. Operators were being eliminated in favor of centralized, computer-assisted dispatching centers, and train orders were being conveyed electronically. (STD) *C&OHS Collection*

Several photos have turned up showing this paint and lettering scheme applied in the 1960s to older C&O steel cabooses. It was an unorthodox application because of the smaller-than-specified monogram and the apparent lack of a red frame stripe. This car has a screen door but the cab below does not. Note the small vent in lower right corner of the side. **(Non-STD)** *Paul Dunn*

Vents in the sides of first-generation steel cabooses were apparently applied with little consistency of size and location. Their purpose was to vent electrical generation equipment, and their location inconsistency may be an indication that C&O officials were experimenting with the installations. The generators were reportedly so noisy that one could not talk on the radio when they were running. Cab 90236 was photographed at Walbridge in April 1963. **(STD)** *Kirk Hise*

This view shows at least a half dozen C&O first-generation cabooses lined up for scrap at Mansbach Metal, Ashland Kentucky, on the banks of the Ohio River. The photo is dated as taken in May 1977. The only car with a visible number, 90291, was placed in Dismantle category at Huntington on March 30, 1977. The late Corky Stanley, a supervisor at Mansbach, became a friend of the author and would make sure to photograph each caboose that came to Mansbach for scrapping, sending us a copy. *Corky Stanley Photo, Collection of Dwight Jones*

The Company's ill-fated program to renumber all C&O cabooses with "C" prefix road numbers had an impact on 90217, shown on the Russell, Kentucky, cab track on September 7, 1980. This car wears the full Chessie System paint scheme (applied at Grand Rapids in June 1976) but the car has not been upgraded and remains for the most part in its original "as built" configuration. Two years later it would be released from Grand Rapids with the modern upgrades given many of this series during that era. *Dwight Jones*

Combination backup lights and FRA markers appeared on virtually all West Virginia and Kentucky mine-run cabooses of this era. Horn applications, as on this car at Raleigh, on April 24, 1982, were rare, though. *Dwight Jones*

Photographed at the Huntington shops on November 6, 1982, while it was there for minor repairs, 90261 carried a self-contained rear end marker/rechargeable battery mounted at floor level. Only a very few markers of this type were used on non-electrified cabooses. *Dwight Jones*

45

A dozen cabooses from the C-20 and C-21 classes are lined up at Peach Creek, West Virginia, on the last Sunday of April 1982. All of the cars have recently been rebuilt and painted at the Grand Rapids shops for assignment to mine-run service. Metal boxes mounted at roof level housed a backup light and **FRA** marker. Tomorrow morning will see this long string of cars gradually thinned as crews once again return to the mines for that seemingly endless supply of black diamonds. Note the splash shields on the end of the 90263. C&O drawing 135-4-503 documented application of those to 90200-series cabooses, with a drawing date of May 10, 1962. However, that drawing superseded an older drawing. *Dwight Jones*

C&O 90229 was outshopped from the Grand Rapids shops on September 12, 1980, after refurbishment and fresh paint. It is shown at Walbridge, Ohio, on September 14, 1980, on its way back to the coalfields. The Transportation Department had assigned it to mine run service out of Shelby, Kentucky. FRA markers were in short supply when this car was completed at Grand Rapids (only a backup light is installed in the roof-mounted light box). The **FRA** light was installed later in the field. Caboose steps often took a beating in derailments and other mishaps. In the case of the first-generation steel cabooses, wood cabooses as well, the steps were cast, so replacements were not available, and if replacement was necessary a fabricated metal step was used such as shown on this car. **(STD)** *Dwight Jones*

A good car shop foreman would save his "dismantle" flat cars—why send an empty flat to a scrap dealer when one could be sent with a scrap load? Caboose 900283, damaged at Cincinnati, and B&O class P-25 flat 8624, built in March 1951, await their trip to the scrapper at the Russell car shops on December 23, 1985. *Dwight Jones*

At the Huntington shops, vandals set the 90261 on fire before it could be repaired for return to service. The burned out hulk was photographed on June 4, 1983. *Dwight Jones*

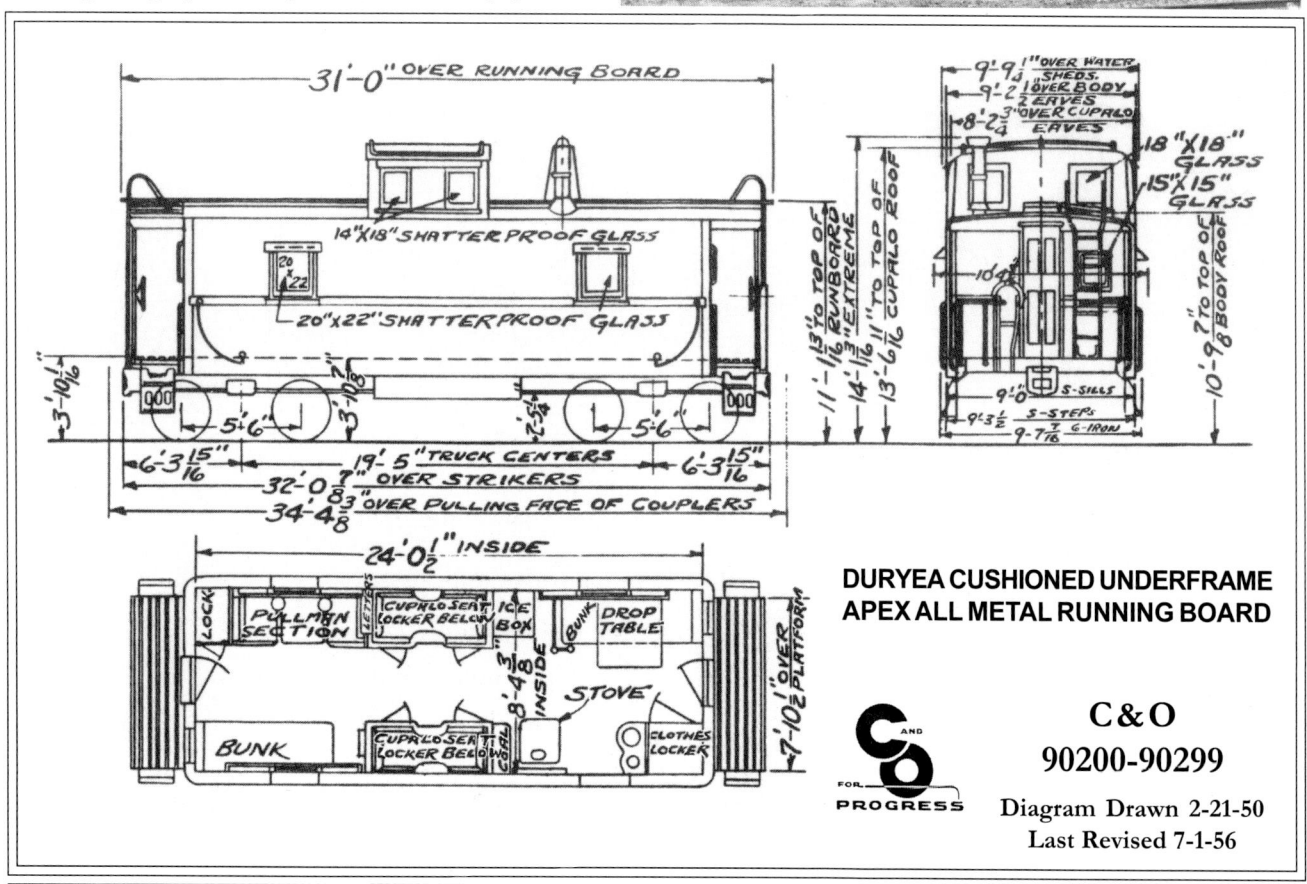

DURYEA CUSHIONED UNDERFRAME
APEX ALL METAL RUNNING BOARD

C&O
90200-90299

Diagram Drawn 2-21-50
Last Revised 7-1-56

47

C&O 900202 is shown at Danville, West Virginia, on April 11, 1987, in assigned minerun service. The conductor who uses this caboose is obviously a West Virginia University fan and is quite proud of the fact. In addition to the large WVU lettering applied on the side under the caboose number, he has trimmed parts of the car in WVU blue including the belt rail along the side and ends of this car. Wonder how he got away with that. Most railroads were somewhat strict with their cabooses, not permitting this type of local "customization". Perhaps his Trainmaster boss also was a big WVU supporter! Another interesting rarity on the C&O is the caboose that is coupled to the 900202, B&O caboose 902953, one of the short-body bay-window cabooses built in the B&O's own shops. *Dwight Jones*

It appears that caboose 90252 has picked a switch at Rainelle, West Virginia. Although wearing Chessie System paint and lettering, this car basically is unmodified from its "as-built" configuration. Through the window one can see a kerosene desk light. This car seems to be heavily damaged, but it was repaired and remained in service for almost 10 years after this December 9, 1979 photo. (STD) *Richard L. Patton, collection of Dwight Jones*

Chapter 9

C&O 90300 Series

As the last few cars of the 90200-series cars were being finished at AC&F's Chicago plant, new 90300-series cars were well underway. Technically both series were built as one single lot (AC&F lot number 3322) but to different General Arrangement drawings. Construction of the two different classes was built as one lot, as can be seen by examining the official build dates. In fact, the last car from the 90200 series carried a build date that has the same month as the first car from the 90300 series.

C&O diagram sheets explain that 90200-series cabooses were for assignment on the Chesapeake District while 90300-series cars were assigned to the Pere Marquette District. The differences between the two series was subtle. Most noticeable was the location of the end ladders, which, on 90300-series cars, were located on the opposite side from ladders found on 90200-series cabooses. Perhaps locating the end ladders on the left side was to standardize cars on the PM District. Pere Marquette's A950- and A800-series cars had ladders mounted on the left side (but other PM cabooses had end ladders mounted on the right side).[2]

Other less noticeable differences concerned interior arrangements and fittings. The PM District cars had the conductor's desk and seat where the washbasin was located in Chesapeake District cabooses. The displaced washbasin on PM District cabs was moved across the aisle to the space occupied by the ice box on Chesapeake District cars. No ice box was identified on diagram sheets for PM District cabooses.

In January 1966 specifications were issued to upgrade interior accommodations of cabooses in the series 90000-90349. See the photos of 90314 and 90346 in this chapter for a description of these changes. It is not known which cars received these modifications.

Many cars in the 90300 series were upgraded at the Grand Rapids shops in 1980 and 1981 along with cars from the 90200 series. Photos in this chapter document those changes as do entries in the roster for this series.

A respectable number of 90300-series cabs were still rostered by the C&O when the original version of this book was published in 1986. With elimination of cabooses, the older cars went first, and since these 90300-series cars still had friction bearing trucks they were all out of service by the mid-1990s. The last car from the series to be retired was the 900321, which was sold to scrap dealer Davidson Lumber in 1996.

The honor of being selected for builder's photos as representative of PM District cars was bestowed on 90314, shown at the AC&F plant in August 1949. C&O would not purchase more "new" cabooses for two decades. (STD) *C&OHS*

49

These end views provide a good comparison showing the differences between Chesapeake District cars (90200s) and the Pere Marquette District cars (90300s). The most obvious difference is the location of the end ladders. Note the glass windows in the door of the 90314. The 90314 also has a chain, to pull the coupler pin, from the end platform, but the 90299 has a long handle to turn the angle cock from the end platform. There does not even appear to be an angle cock on the 90314. Note that both of these cars are equipped with screen doors. *C&OHS Collection*

Proof that new FRA windows are indeed missile-proof is provided by 900336 at the Huntington car shops on November 22, 1984. Application of the caboose number over the end window was nonstandard. The roof box housed the backup light (on the left) and an amber-colored FRA light. Some of the updated modifications on this car include the long "T" handle shown in its storage position just to the right of the ladder (it could be used to turn the angle cock when standing on the end platform), application of splash shields applied to the end railings, and replacement of the safety chain (just to the right of the brake wheel) with a fixed safety rod. *Dwight Jones*

Many C&O steel cabooses have their numbers steel-stamped on a lower corner in 1/2" high characters as on 900304 at Russell on December 31, 1986. *Dwight Jones*

50   Steel Cabooses of the Chesapeake & Ohio

A string of five freshly-completed 90300-series cars prepares to leave the American Car & Foundry plant at Chicago in 1949. Builders typically release new cars in groups rather than a single car at a time. **(STD)** *C&OHS Collection*

Caboose 90346, probably photographed around 1970, and 90314, photographed at Walbridge on December 15, 1969, are examples of cars that have had their interiors upgraded as mentioned in previous chapters. January 21, 1966, is the date carried on C&O Mechanical Department drawing 139-2-709, which documented the changes that were to be made to C&O cabooses in series 90001-90349. Those changes called for replacement of the coal stove with an oil-burning unit, elimination of the coal box, addition of a 30-gallon oil tank, addition of a new refrigerator and water cooler, elimination of the old ice box, addition of a new 30-gallon water tank, removal of the old water tank, and addition of an axle-driven alternator, a battery, electric lights and safety glass. In these two photos, the aluminum sash windows, long vent pipe for the new toilet compartment, and oil fill spout (on 90346) are all visible. Note that the cupola side windows were applied differently to these two cars. The window on 90314 conforms to the slight slope of the cupola side while the window on 90346 has been recessed so that it will be in a vertical plane. *Paul Dunn and Kirk Hise*

51

C&O 90340 is shown at Walbridge, Ohio, on February 18, 1969. Mounted to the cupola roof is a mini-windmill, which is really turning on this day. The photographer indicated that this was a device installed by the railroad to generate electricity for the caboose. It was reported to still be on the caboose in early 1972, although the interior electrical equipment had been removed by that date. Reportedly this type of device also was used on SAL and FEC cabooses. Obviously this is some type of early electrical experiment as the railroad searched for ways to generate the power needed for radio use as well as interior lighting. *Kirk Hise*

Four 90300-series cabooses were sold to C&O subsidiary Chicago South Shore and South Bend in two lots—two in 1974 and two in 1976. The CSS&SB retained the C&O yellow paint and last three road-number digits, adding a red South Shore Line monogram. Cab 329 was photographed at Michigan City, Indiana, October 8, 1982. In 1985 CSS&SB retired their four ex-C&O cabs. *Dwight Jones*

52   Steel Cabooses of the Chesapeake & Ohio

C&O 90347 was photographed in full Chessie System paint at Silver Grove, Kentucky, on April 4, 1980. The car shows little modification from its as-built appearance with exception of the addition of the standard C&O swivel reflectorized marker panels. This car last was painted at the Huntington shops in October 1977. Even so, it would be heading to the Grand Rapids shops next year for another Chessie coat. (STD) *Dwight Jones*

Caboose 90340 was shown on the previous page with a special roof-mounted windmill. That same car is shown here as the worst-looking caboose on the Chessie System when photographed at Columbus on February 8, 1986. Something caused the paint to peel from the body down to bare metal, which then rusted. Perhaps the roof-mounted generator was not the only experiment C&O was carrying out on this car. It was retired nine months after this photo was taken. *Dwight Jones*

Walbridge, Ohio, was home base for many upgraded 90200- and 90300-series cabooses that were assigned there for yard and transfer service after wood cabooses were phased out. Lack of electric power distinguished these cars from other upgraded cabooses in the same series, which were assigned to minerun service. The cars in this string all have fresh paint and have been rehabilitated at the Grand Rapids shops where they were given new FRA windows and had their window awnings removed. *Dwight Jones*

C&O 90300-90349

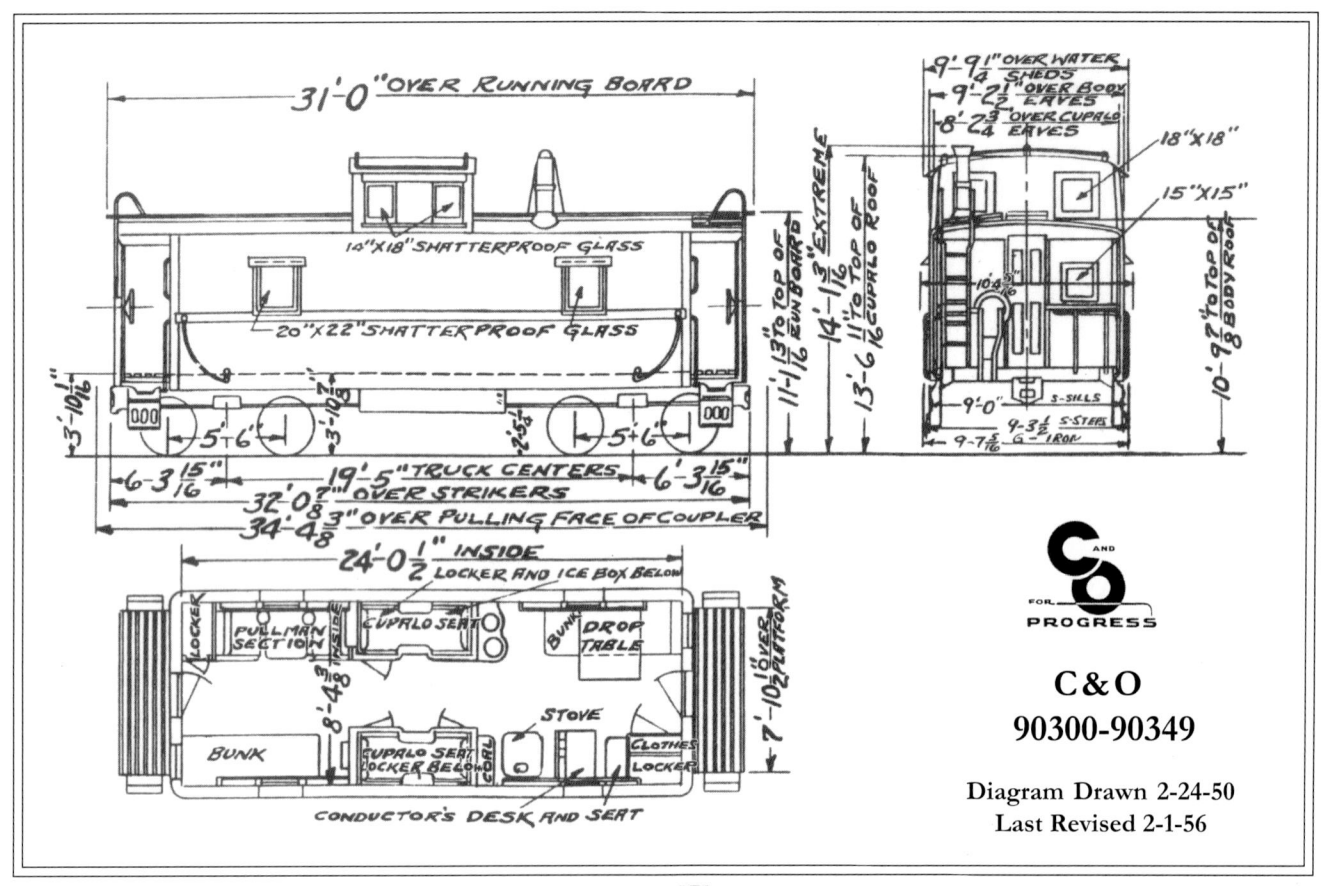

Diagram Drawn 2-24-50
Last Revised 2-1-56

C&O caboose 90340 was pictured earlier in this chapter with its nomination as the worst looking caboose on the Chessie System. As might have been expected, its days were numbered. The car is shown here on September 30, 1987, being scrapped at Parsons Yard, Columbus. After setting the body off its trucks, the next step typically was to burn away the wood interior leaving a metal hulk which scrappers then would cut up with torches. Modern day restrictions on burning, particularly in urban areas, eliminated this practice. *Dwight Jones*

C&O 90308 shares the Queensgate cab track on the last day of 1982 with one-of-a-kind box car conversion C3051. The oddball was the prototype for a design intended to be a cost-effective replacement for aging wood cabooses used in yard, transfer, and mine-run service. No additional cars of this type ever were completed. *Dwight Jones*

Steel Cabooses of the Chesapeake & Ohio

Chapter 10

Experimental Conversions

In the mid-1950s some strange scribblings of caboose car designs were being made in Cleveland. It was happening in the office of the Director of Design, Public Relations Department. That office apparently had been requested to examine the current C&O caboose design with an eye toward developing a new, state-of-the art design that could be retrofitted to the existing caboose fleet.

At Richmond, Virginia, the C&O Mechanical Department also was working on a new design for caboose cars—one, also, that could be retrofitted to older caboose cars then in service. Although there is evidence that the designers in Cleveland were working with the engineers in Richmond, their concepts were quite different. The Cleveland tracings indicate concepts that favored aerodynamic renditions that modeled elements of "spacecraft" (keep in mind that this was the 1950s!). Mechanical Department personnel in Richmond favored a much simpler, pragmatic, down-to-earth design.

As early as April 1956, the Mechanical Department engineers completed drawing 136-11-1804, which called for steel sheathing to be applied to two C&O wood-sheathed cabooses. Cars 90667 and 90680 were given steel sheathing in 1956.

Not totally satisfied, the designers and mechanical staff kept at their work, and in 1957 the third wood-sheathed caboose was retrofitted with steel sheathing. The design was different from the first two in that it featured a permanent bay extension to the cupola sides. Nearly two years after that third conversion was completed, a fourth car emerged from C&O shops. This car featured yet another variation—the cupola bay had been extended down the side of the carbody, making this car a true extended vision caboose and a forerunner of future purchases of the same type of caboose from ICC..

No additional cars ever received the conversion treatment. A fifth car was apparently scheduled to receive steel sheathing—its number was even listed on the C&O diagram sheet—but it never was converted. The conversion program came to a halt—a program that had covered more than three years and saw the conversion of only four cabooses using three different body styles.

Fresh out of the Raceland paint shop, 90675 poses for a builder's photo in July 1957. The yellow caboose scheme is only one year old, and safety appliances, end railings, ladders, and steps are painted green. This car was the third of the four cars converted to steel and exhibits the extended cupola design. (STD) *C&OHS Collection*

55

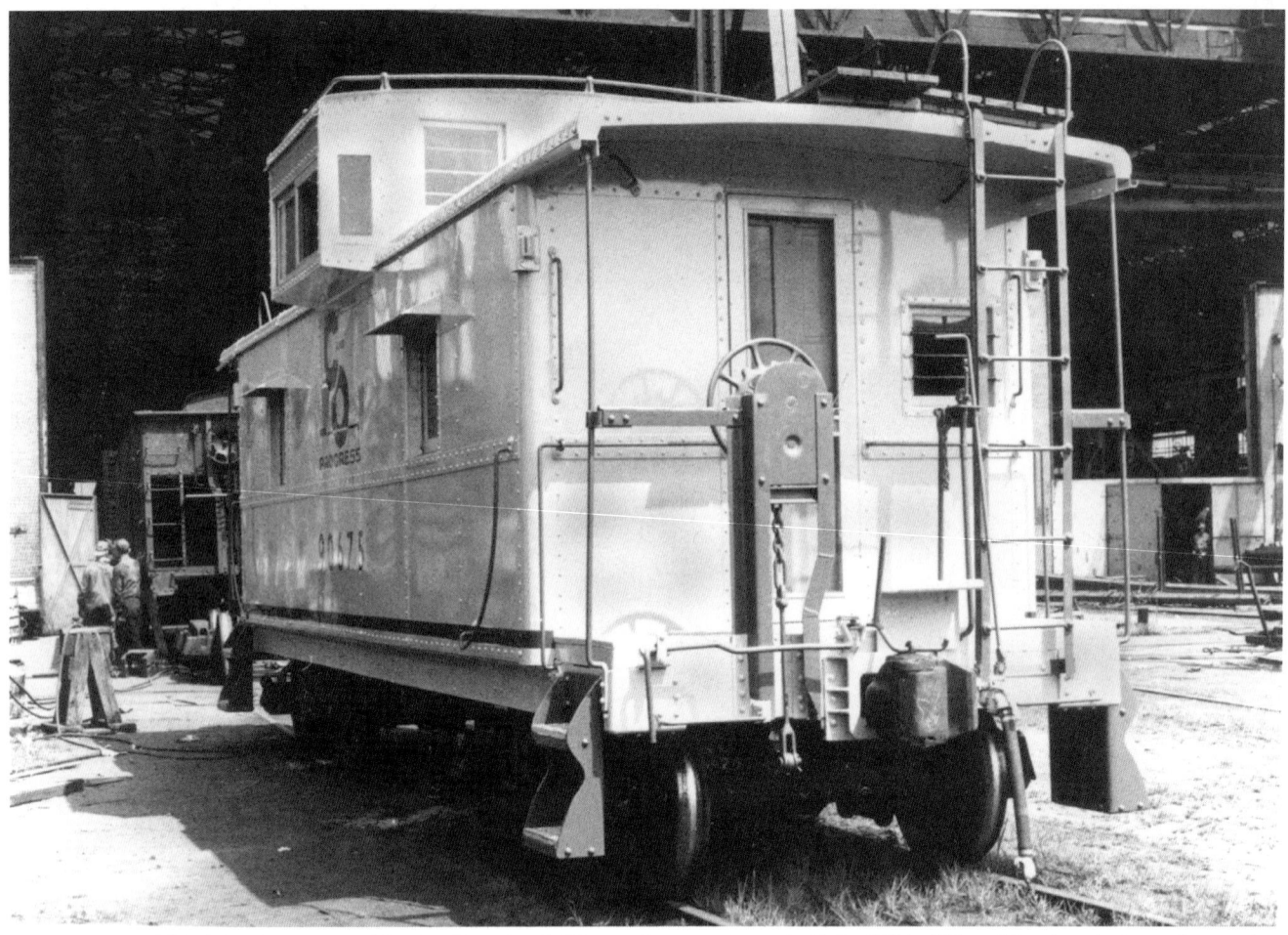

A completed 90675 is shown outside the Raceland, Kentucky, carshops in July 1957. The side view below shows the oversize cupola side windows. New fabricated steps have been fashioned to match the standard C&O cast steps found on other steel cabooses. The photo above shows the safety rods applied on the outside of the platform end window and on the inside of the cupola end windows. The purpose of these was to prevent someone from being ejected in case of an emergency brake application. *C&O Historical Society collection*

This end view of the 90675, taken at Raceland in 1957, provides a good look at the extended cupola bay. Note that the wood running boards were retained. Being that the bug season is at hand, the car is equipped with a screen door. **(STD)** *C&OHS Collection*

The 90675 was in service at Plymouth, Michigan, for a long time in the mid-1960s.

After its 1957 conversion, 90675 was listed for a short time as a "Research Test Caboose". The car has been extensively outfitted for data collection, as evidenced by the electrical cables strung along the car, the wood box on the roof, and the technician on the end platform who appears to be tinkering with an air compressor. Letters stenciled on each side identified "A" and "B" ends. **(STD)** *C&OHS Collection*

57

C&O 90667 was the first of the four experimental conversions of the mid-1950s. The car is shown in service at Walbridge, Ohio, on June 15, 1976, coupled to a B&O I-5 family caboose. The car was in restricted yard service, as indicated by the "R" stencilled on the side, due to its age—it had 52 years of service under its belt when this photo was taken. The car wears the simplified "Walbridge Scheme", a Chessie scheme so named because it was the Walbridge shops that applied this simplified scheme to many wood and first-generation steel cabooses. *Howard W. Ameling*

Not much time is left for C&O cabooses 90273 and experimental 90667. The two were photographed on June 29, 1980, at scrap dealer Portsmouth Iron & Metal, Portsmouth, Ohio. *Dwight Jones*

The city of Grant, Michigan, acquired the 90680 for display in the downtown area. This night photo was made there on September 4, 1983. The underbody battery box identifies this car as having full electric power. That work was completed at the Grand Rapids shops on November 22, 1980. The car was last painted at the Huntington car shops in June 1977. The 90680 was used on the Saginaw to Port Huron local in the early 1950s. *Dwight Jones*

Wearing fresh paint, 90665 was on a transfer run to the D&TSL's Lang Yard in northern Toledo when Kirk Hise photographed it on October 3, 1970. Less than two years later it was wrecked and was put in "Dismantle" category where it remained for over eight years. At left, the car is shown on display at Huntington, West Virginia, at the C.P. Huntington Railroad Historical Society's railroad park awaiting restoration. The car is shown below on November 29, 2008, after restoration, which included repairing the sideswipe damage shown in the middle photo. *Bottom two photos, Dwight Jones*

59

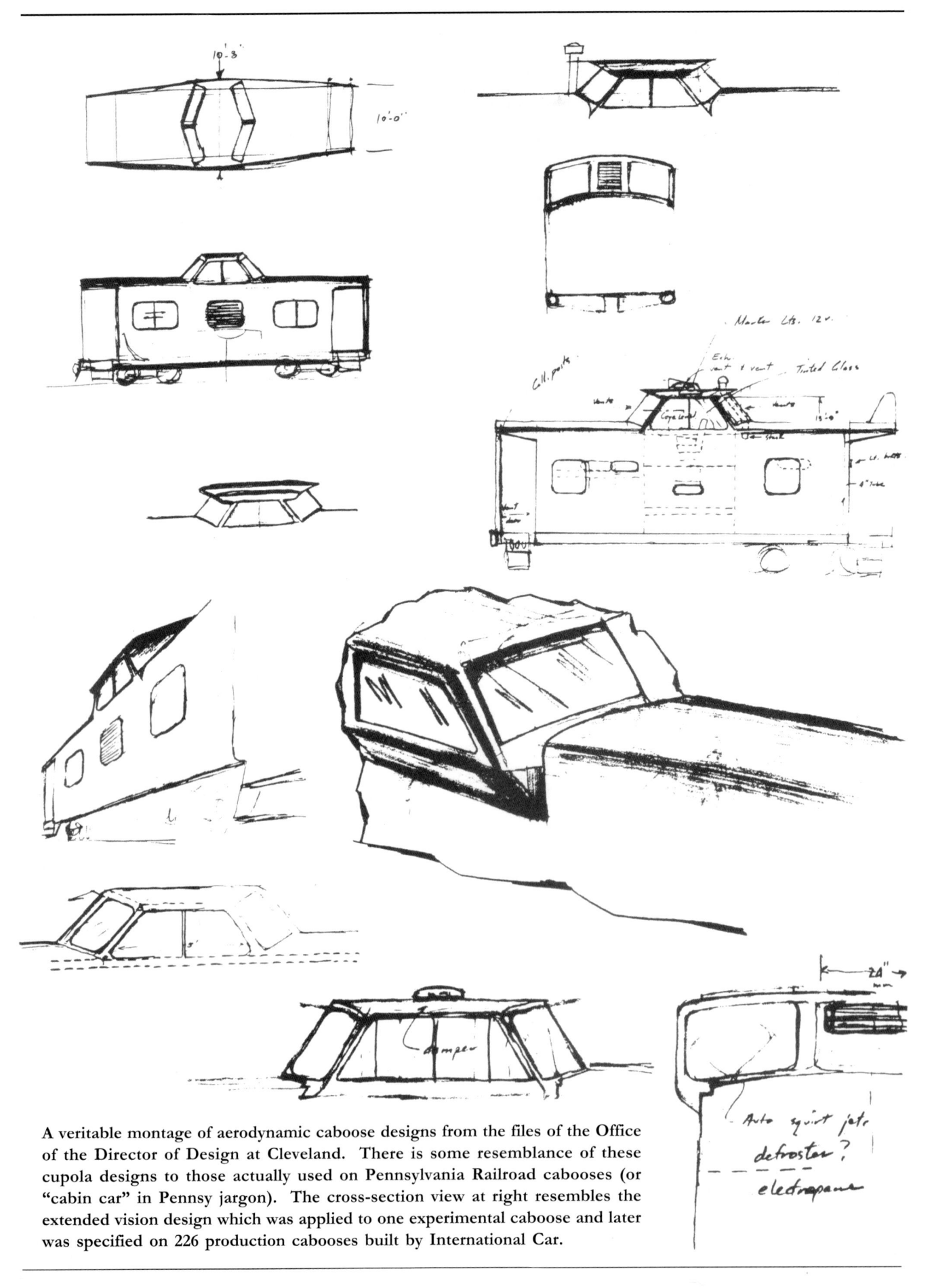

A veritable montage of aerodynamic caboose designs from the files of the Office of the Director of Design at Cleveland. There is some resemblance of these cupola designs to those actually used on Pennsylvania Railroad cabooses (or "cabin car" in Pennsy jargon). The cross-section view at right resembles the extended vision design which was applied to one experimental caboose and later was specified on 226 production cabooses built by International Car.

60   Steel Cabooses of the Chesapeake & Ohio

C&O Experimental Conversions Roster

No.	Date Built	Converted to Steel	Body Type	Retired	Disposition / 1983 Location / Notes
90665	5-3-24	5- -59	Extended Vision	11- -80	Wrk'd: WAL 7-30-72; donated 12-16-80 to C.P. Huntington Chapter NRHS
90667	5-3-24	7-9-56	Standard Cupola	11- -79	Sold 11-6-79 to scrap dealer Portsmouth Iron & Metal, Portsmouth, OH
90669	5-8-24	none	not converted	11-10-72	Sold: Nordson Foundation Amherst, Ohio, for display
90675	5-17-24	7-15-57	Cupola with Bay	4- -71	Sold 2-22-71 to scrap dealer Mansbach Metal, Ashland, KY
90680	5-17-24	12- -56	Standard Cupola	2- -82	Sold 5-20-83 to city of Grant, MI, and placed on public display

More on C&O 90675

Caboose 90675, when initially outshopped, was scheduled for display at various locations around the C&O in order that company officers get feedback from employees on the reconditioned caboose. The cab was moved from Russell to Columbus on August 15, 1957, where it was to be displayed and then forwarded to Walbridge not later than Saturday morning, August 17. After the display at Columbus, a letter was issued that reviewed comments from those employees who had an opportunity to inspect this caboose. The letter, dated August 15, 1957, is reproduced below:

"Caboose 90675 arrived Parsons on No. 195 from Russell, Kentucky, August 15 and was placed on stub 19 until early A.M. of August 17. While at Parsons many of our employees had the opportunity of viewing this caboose. Their comments were many and varied, some liking one particular feature better than others.

"The safety belts in the cupola were not received very enthusiastically by the employees. Some thought it was an excellent idea but said they did not want to be strapped in the cupola should the train go into emergency and the caboose derail.

"There was not much comment regarding the bunk cushions being bolted so that they would be held in place, thereby preventing the cushions and the men from sliding off the seat boxes in case of a rough stop.

"All the employees liked the shatterproof, or safety, glass in the cupola windows.

"The overhead rod installed along the ceiling the length of the caboose was received with very little enthusiasm as a great number of our employees stated they did not want to be in a position of hanging onto this rod after the caboose was involved in any type of rough stop.

"The general opinion of the employees was that they all liked the open metal grating steps but did not care for this grating on the rear platform, feeling it would become clogged with snow and ice in winter; therefore making it impossible to sweep the ice and snow from between the grating.

"They liked the non-spin vertical hand brake and the foot brace under the desk and the fact that all desk corners were rounded. It was the general opinion of most of the employees that the guard rail placed around the stove to provide a hand hold would be useless; however if it were adopted it should be placed in such a manner as not to protrude into the aisle-way as it does on caboose 90675. The men were well pleased with the cupboard space.

"Contrary to my expectations, very few of our employees were impressed with the wide cupola. Most of the employees observed that the caboose was not a Duryea underframe and expressed the opinion that they would be sorely disappointed with any new caboose purchased unless it was of the Duryea underframe construction.

"In the past week since the caboose was on exhibition here, I have talked with a great many of our older trainmen and they have summed their feelings up in this manner: If the railway company wants to do anything for the men in the way of improvements on cabooses they would like to have foam rubber cushions and Estate square stoves in all their cabooses and retain the cabooses they have at the present time. Conductors H.H. Blosser, D.J. Humphrey and W.J. Keiper came to my office and stated that there is nothing wrong with their present cabooses as they are; they are the best we have had for years; they would like to keep them and they would appreciate the installation of foam rubber cushions and Estate square stoves."

The above letter was signed by C. E. Chesher, Trainmaster, Hocking Division.

C&O
90665-90680

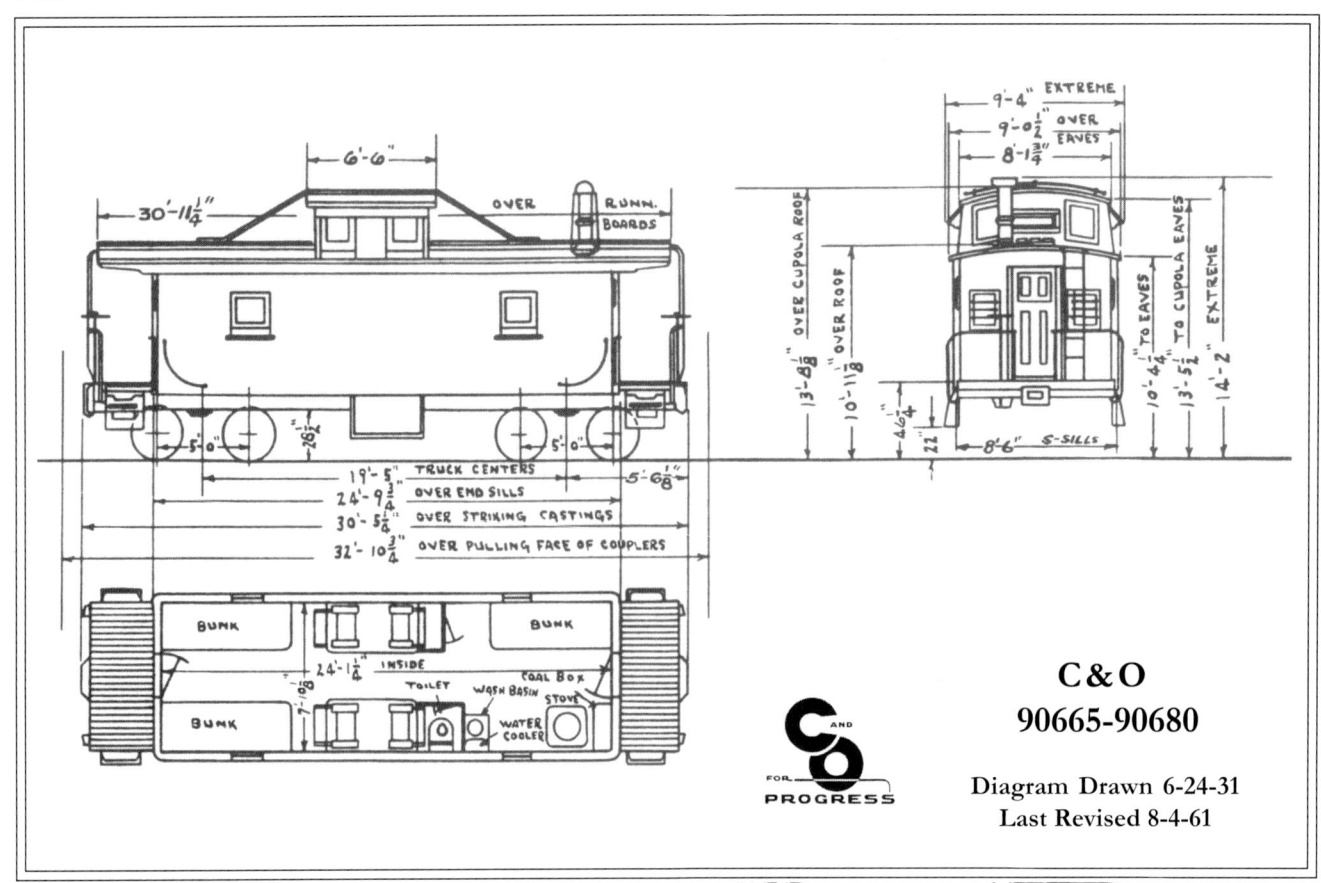

Diagram Drawn 6-24-31
Last Revised 8-4-61

Historians might never have known that only four cabooses, and not five as indicated on the C&O diagram sheet, were converted to steel if it had not been for the fact that the fifth car, 90669, was preserved. It was acquired by the Nordson Foundation and is displayed at Amherst, Ohio, with C&O caboose 90697 and C&O passenger cars 2612 and 1653. Photographed on February 4, 1983, the car had completed the restoration process, but lacked its first road-number digit. *Dwight Jones*

Steel Cabooses of the Chesapeake & Ohio

Chapter 11

C&O 90350 Series

The only steel cabooses acquired secondhand by the C&O (until a later acquisition of four Toledo Terminal cabooses), were a handful of former Western Maryland cars purchased in late 1965. It seems odd that a railroad that rostered as many cabooses as did C&O (723 cars in 1965) would be helped much by the addition of only seven cabooses. In fact, the seven acquisitions would account for less than one percent of the total C&O caboose fleet! In any event, either they must have been priced too low to pass up, or C&O desperately needed a few steel cabs for specific yard and transfer service assignments.

The design of these cabooses was one of the most famous of any cupola caboose. Credit for the original design has been given to the Mechanical Department of the Reading Railroad, which initially developed the cars to meet the rigid safety requirements of the state of New York. Reading built its first cars in 1924 and built several lots thereafter at their Reading, Pennsylvania, shops. The design was eventually picked up by a number of lines and became a favorite among northeastern railroads. Other first-time users included Jersey Central, Lehigh & Hudson River, Lehigh Valley, Pittsburgh & West Virginia, and Lehigh & New England. A large number of the cabooses originally owned by first-time users later wound up on other lines, further attesting to the well-founded design.[9]

Western Maryland owned a total of 105 cabooses of this design, which were WM class NE. The cars were assembled at the Western Maryland shops at Hagerstown, Maryland, between 1936 and 1940 from kits supplied by Bethlehem Steel Company. The seven cars acquired by C&O were part of a total of 26 cabooses (over a fourth of the entire WM caboose fleet!) that Western Maryland removed from service between 1962 and 1966.

C&O's seven ex-Western Maryland cabooses were sent to the Raceland shops for modification soon after acquisition. C&O-style "tender" steps were added, window awnings were applied over the side windows, and some changes were made to grab irons and railings on the ends of the cars. It is interesting to note that two of the cars in this group eventually became the oldest steel cabooses on the C&O.

The seven former Western Maryland cabooses acquired by the C&O averaged just over 26 years old when obtained, and hence spent most of their active lives in assigned yard and transfer service. Most of the cars seemed to congregate at either Walbridge or Chicago, where they could be used in less demanding service. By early 1986 the three remaining former WM cabs were in bad-order storage. Fortunately one of the cars has been saved, as is shown later in this chapter.

This C&O builder's photo shows the first of the Western Maryland conversions at the Raceland carshops in early 1966. Note the lack of a red side stripe and the grossly offset C&O monogram. The Raceland shops has a long history of poor paint and lettering practices. *C&OHS Collection*

Western Maryland 1808 was in fresh red paint when W. Raymond Hicks made this photo at Maryland Junction on August 20, 1946. These cars originally did not have end windows, which later were added by WM. This car became C&O 90351 in 1966. *W. Raymond Hicks*

An end view of C&O 90350 taken at Walbridge, Ohio, on March 20, 1982, shows end details on these former Western Maryland cabooses. C&O added "tender" steps, and sealed one end window due to adding a locker on the interior at this location. End railings also were modified. And of course the car was equipped with the standard C&O reflectorized swivel markers. *Dwight Jones*

For more information on Western Maryland cabooses, refer to the books shown on page 144.

A bright sunny day at Walbridge, on October 23, 1982, found 900350 sitting virtually by itself in the yard. Diagonally striped, reflectorized end panels were applied only to cabooses assigned to the C&O's Toledo Terminal. The leaf springs have been replaced with coil springs on the far truck. *Dwight Jones*

An aerial look at 90356 at Barr Yard in Chicago on May 29, 1983, offers a good view of the roof construction. **(STD)** *Dwight Jones*

C&O cabooses assigned to the Chicago Terminal had large sections of their side repainted to remove the C&O monogram before renumbering to the six-digit road numbers, as on 900356, photographed at Chicago on August 31, 1984. No other location removed the old monogram when applying the new numbers. *Dwight Jones*

Photographed at Walbridge on July 26, 1980, 90351 has been given both a "C" prefix to its road number, and an "R" suffix. The suffix denotes a "Restricted" car. In this case, 90351 was restricted due to trucks, underframe, and draft gear. *Dwight Jones*

C&O 90355 was involved in a system accident and subsequently was placed into "Dismantle" category. The car was photographed in the bad order storage line at the Grand Rapids shops on July 3, 1982. It had been stenciled as a "Hold for Dismantle" in December 1977, hence it has been in storage for five years. The car later was moved to Russell, Kentucky, and from there it was sold to nearby scrap dealer Mansbach Metal at Ashland. *Dwight Jones*

The last Western Maryland caboose left in service on CSX, 901863, was acquired in 2004 by the Hagerstown Roundhouse Museum and, after refurbishment into the WM's famous "speed lettering" scheme, was placed on display at the group's museum in Hagerstown.

Only one of the former Western Maryland C&O cabooses was saved from the scrapper. The 90352 is shown on display at Sandusky, Ohio, on May 7, 1983. The car was later moved to another display location along the north side of the Ohio Turnpike near Milan, Ohio. The property now is part of the Metro Parks of Erie County. *Dwight Jones*

C&O 90353 is shown on April 2, 1968, at "D" Yard in Walbridge, Ohio. The left side window has been covered with yellow during the last repainting. *Kirk Hise*

The 90355 (at left) is accompanied by A969 (center) and 900956 at Russell, Kentucky, on September 1, 1985. The trio was enroute to scrapper Mansbach Metal at Ashland. *Dwight Jones*

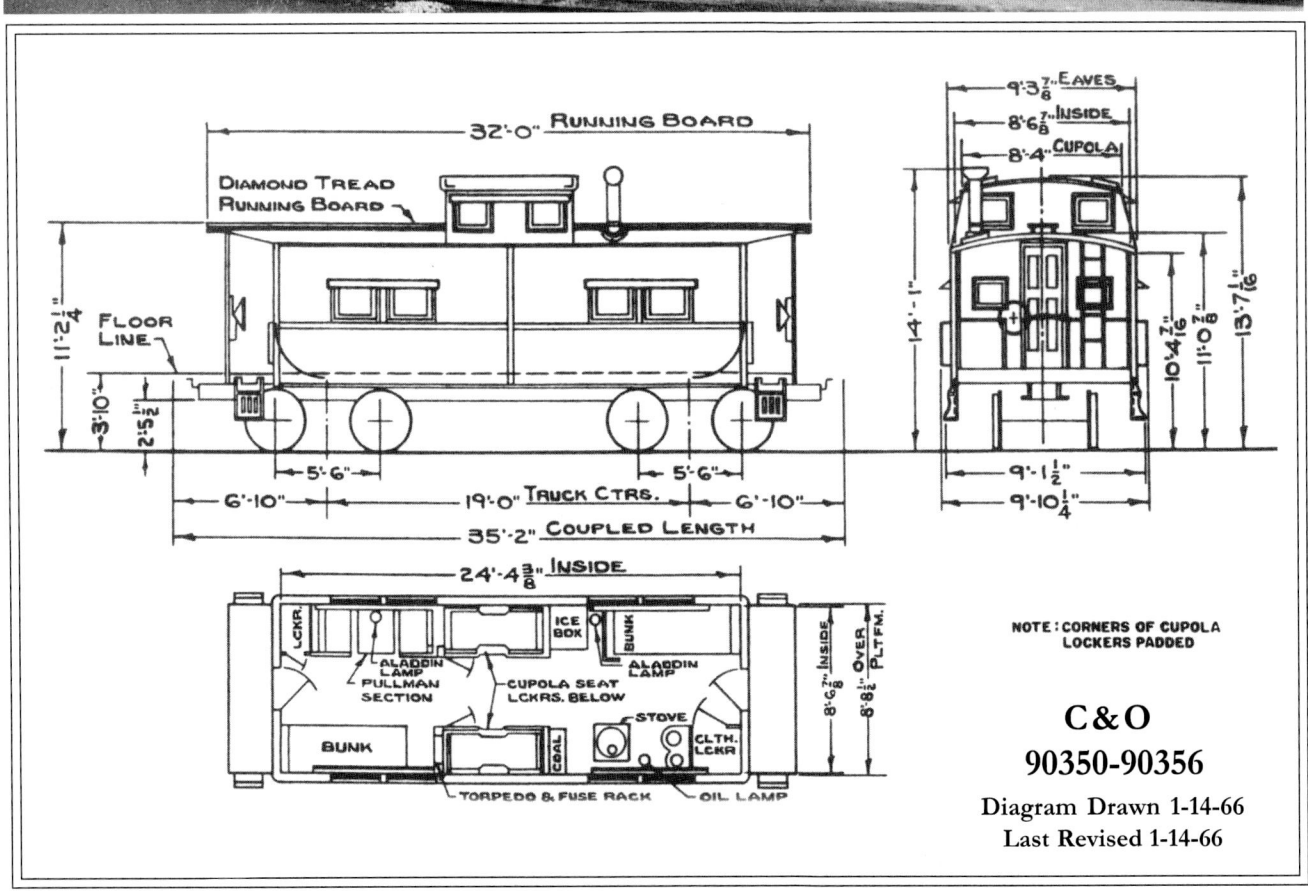

NOTE: CORNERS OF CUPOLA LOCKERS PADDED

**C&O
90350-90356**

Diagram Drawn 1-14-66
Last Revised 1-14-66

67

Chapter 12

C&O 3100-3325 Series

In 1968 C&O officials placed an order with the International Car Company of Kenton, Ohio, for new caboose cars. At that time the total quantity of cabooses in service on the C&O had declined to the lowest number in the steel caboose era. This new order for 100 cabooses would bolster the sagging fleet and allow for the retirement of a few more wooden veterans. Other than the small handful of former Western Maryland cabs acquired in 1965, which had minimal impact on the overall fleet, it had been nearly two decades since the last new cabooses had arrived on the property.

Although the C&O had a long history of purchasing cabooses from car builders, this was the first order placed with International Car. This group of cabooses was notable in a number of other respects as well. They were the first of the extended vision cupola design to be purchased new, the first to feature all-welded carbodies, and the first to ride on roller-bearing trucks.[10]

Their state-of-the-art construction was secondary to more obvious changes in both the paint scheme and the numbering system. Yellow was out, blue was in. And what happened to the standard caboose numbering system of five digits? C&O fans would fret, but in time both the yellow paint and '90' caboose number prefixes would return.

Standardized C&O/B&O paint and lettering schemes were being adopted in the late 1960s for all freight equipment, and cabooses were no exception. The blue adopted for caboose cars was a stark contrast to the old yellow image, and there are many different thoughts as why blue was selected for cabooses (see chapter 10). The new C&O four-digit caboose road numbers were assigned in sequence with the B&O caboose numbering system, which dated to the early 1900s. New B&O cabooses had last been delivered in 1965-66 with road numbers in the C3000 series. So it was not all that illogical to see new C&O cabooses begin with the 3100 series.

The original order for 100 cabooses was supplemented with an additional 60 cars delivered in 1969, 55 more delivered in 1970, and a final 11 cars built in 1971.

It is interesting to speculate that, if the new caboose numbering system had not been adopted for these cabooses, they

The first "new" caboose for C&O in nearly 20 years, and the first cab in the blue paint scheme was photographed at the International Car Company plant in 1968. Midget electric marker lights came standard on these cars. This high elevation view provides a good look at the ladder handholds on the roof and the roof running boards which only appeared on the first 160 cars. Soon 3100 would be off to its assigned location at Peru, Indiana. (STD) *C&O Railway*

probably would have been numbered in series 90358-90583, since it was standard C&O practice not to skip road numbers between different classes of cabooses.

The 226 cars were virtually identical except for the absence of roof running boards and end ladders on cars numbered 3260 and higher. That government-mandated safety feature applied to freight cars as well as cabooses. Many freight cars were later modified to eliminate the accident-prone roof running boards and end ladders. Cabooses on the C&O later were modified only on a very random and limited basis.

When delivered, these new cabooses were assigned, in groups, to specific areas of the C&O. We have attempted to reconstruct the original assignments of these cabs based on personal observations, company data, and photo locations. Their original assignments appear to have been as follows:

3100-3119 Peru, Indiana
3120-3162 Grand Rapids, Michigan
3163-3178 Saginaw, Michigan
3179-3187 Silver Grove, Kentucky
3188-3195 Richmond, Virginia
3196-3199 Peru, Indiana
3200-3215 Clifton Forge, Virginia
3216-3223 Richmond, Virginia
3224-3233 Clifton Forge, Virginia
3234-3236 Hinton, West Virginia
3237-3245 Russell, Kentucky
3246-3248 Columbus, Ohio
3249-3252 Russell, Kentucky
3253-3259 Virginia Division
3260-3274 Michigan Division
3275-3288 Columbus, Ohio
3289-3299 Russell, Kentucky
3300-3308 Hinton, West Virginia
3309-3313 Russell, Kentucky
3314-3320 Michigan Division
3321-3325 Columbus, Ohio

As the years passed, caboose surpluses and shortages at various locations resulted in transfers of some cabooses to other locales. The gradual implementation of system-wide caboose pooling, inaugurated in the early 1980s, removed the final barrier to truly integrating the fleet.

Test Generators

C&O extended vision cabooses 3138 and 3160 were specially equipped with end-of-axle alternators for testing on the Chesapeake & Ohio Railway. A March 12, 1973, internal company memo indicated the following:

"The original alternators, drive shafts and gear units have been

A bird's-eye view shows cabooses 903162 and 903533 as seen from the yardmaster's perch in aptly named "C&O High Tower" at Columbus, Ohio, on March 13, 1983. *Dwight Jones*

removed from both cars and the new style combination drive and alternator have been mounted on R-2 journal box with seven (7) retaining bolts.

"Please arrange to have this equipment on both caboose cars inspected daily for any defects, this inspection shall include voltage and gravity readings.

"All information regarding these two units shall be recorded on Form L-723.

"The proper oil level in the gear unit must be maintained and the coupling shaft to be lubricated at 30-day intervals. Refer to Freight Circular CD-38 for proper trip inspection, also observing the portable cable attached to the alternator for any wear against the truck side frame."

Any defects to the test electrical equipment was to be reported "at once" to the Huntington mechanical offices.

These tests apparently proved satisfactory as photos show quite a number of these cabooses were modified with this type of equipment in later years.

Pooling of Cabooses

An agreement signed between the C&O Railway and the Order of Railway Conductors and Brakemen allowed for the pooling of cabooses on certain sections of the C&O. This agreement detailed specific criteria that cabooses had to meet in order to qualify them for pool service. This had direct bearing on the purchase of the extended vision cupola cabooses from International Car as well as the rebuilding of older cabs into the 3500 and 3600-series. The agreement was signed with the Trainmen March 27, 1968, and with the Conductors June 4, 1968. Details of the agreement are reproduced below.

NATIONAL MEDIATION BOARD

MEDIATION AGREEMENT

ORDER OF RAILWAY CONDUCTORS AND BRAKE-MEN

and

THE CHESAPEAKE AND OHIO RAILWAY COMPANY
EASTERN AND CENTRAL REGIONS
AND HOCKING DIVISION

In settlement of differences as set forth in an application for mediation as described in Docket Case A-8233 of the National Mediation Board and under the provisions of the Railway Labor Act, Amended, it is mutually agreed that the questions so submitted by the said Chesapeake and Ohio Railway Company and the Order of Railway Conductors and Brakemen shall be and hereby disposed of as contained in the agreement between the parties, copy of which is attached hereto but not made part hereof.

This Agreement shall become effective June 4, 1968, and remain in effect thereafter subject to provisions of the Railway Labor Act, Amended.

Agreement signed at Huntington, West Virginia, this 4th day of June, 1968.

[the letter was signed by a representative of the Chesapeake and Ohio Railway Company, a Vice President of the Order of Railway Conductors and Brakemen, and the National Mediation Board representative.]

The actual agreement referred to in the above letter is reproduced below:

MEMORANDUM AGREEMENT BETWEEN THE CHESAPEAKE AND OHIO RAILWAY COMPANY AND EMPLOYEES REPRESENTED BY THE ORDER OF RAILWAY CONDUCTORS AND BRAKEMEN

Effective June 4, 1968

It is agreed that effective as of the date of this agreement, the Carrier has the right to pool and/or run through cabooses in all classes of service; provided, however, if the Carrier elects to pool cabooses on a particular Division or seniority district and/or run cabooses through over two or more Division or seniority districts, the following conditions will apply:

1.   In other than minerun (shifter) territory, cabooses that are pooled and/or run through will either be existing cabooses "rebuilt" to include the features shown below or new cabooses built to these specifications:

> Cupolas
> Stabilized trucks
> Steel wheels
> Vertical gear hand brakes
> Adequately cushioned center sill
> Safety steps
> Safety glass in windows
> Insulation for floor, sides and roof
> Electric lights and markers
> Toilets - stainless steel
> Lavatory - stainless steel
> Bunks
> Foam rubber cushions 4" thick
> Screens on windows and doors
> Automatic oil heater with separate oil tank
> Ice box
> Lockers

Mirror
Water cooler

2. In minerun (shifter) territory, cabooses may be pooled in minerun (shifter) service in any pool or pools in such territory, provided steel cabooses are furnished, painted and completely rehabilitated to specifications of caboose cars 90200-90299, copy attached [a standard diagram sheet of the 90200-series cars was attached—dej]. Such cabooses will not be used by crews in other than minerun (shifter) territory.

3. The Carrier will have cabooses which are pooled and/or run through supplied with the following in addition to supplies required by the Carrier:

Paper cups and cup dispenser
Paper towels and towel dispenser
Hand soap
Fuel
Water
Ice
Stationery
Toilet paper
First Aid kit

4. Conductors will give advance notice of the need for stationery, supplies, etc., on cabooses to the end that such items may be replenished. A supply check list will be made available for this purpose.

5. Cabooses will be kept clean and in a sanitary condition by the Company; however, crews will cooperate in keeping cabooses clean during the time they are occupying them. Caboose water tanks will be flushed and cleaned at regular intervals of not more than three (3) months.

6. Conductors using pooled cabooses will not be required to leave terminal with a caboose which is not clean and supplied as provided herein, or in proper condition. Conductors may report a caboose as unfit and the deficiencies will be corrected or unsatisfactory caboose replaced with one in proper condition, and crew operated in proper turn.

7. Conductors using pooled caboose cars will not be held responsible for their cabooses not being properly supplied.

8. The terminals and the points within such terminals between which transportation will be furnished will be agreed upon between the Director of Labor Relations and the General Chairman or their designated representatives before the pooling of cabooses is made effective.

9. At the away-from-home terminals for employees whose cabooses are pooled and/or run through, lockers of steel construction, size 18" deep x 21" wide x 78" high, will be provided to accommodate the normal wearing of apparel and personal effects of the employees.

10. Locker rooms and washing facilities, but not including shower bath facilities, will be provided by the Carrier at the home terminal for use of employees whose cabooses are pooled and/or run through. The lockers, size 18" deep x 21" wide x 78" high, will be of steel construction to accommodate the normal wearing apparel and personal effects of the employees.

11. Conductors using pooled caboose cars will be paid an expense allowance of 1 cent a mile with a minimum of $1.00 for each trip (terminal to terminal), including deadhead trips on freight trains. This expense allowance will not be changed without agreement between the parties. This expense allowance will not be used in determining earnings for purpose of regulating the working list under Rule 46 or Article 25 on the Hocking Division.

12. The carrier may completely pool cabooses in any particular freight pool or pools or any set of regular assignments as soon as sufficient cabooses as specified in Section 1 or 2 are available to fully protect the particular service involved and the provisions of Section 8 of this agreement are agreed upon. The General Chairman will be given thirty (30) days' advance notice as to the date on which the pooling arrangement is to be made effective, specifying the territory and service involved, and appropriate notice will also be posted to the employees affected.

This agreement signed at Huntington, West Virginia, this 4th day of June, 1968, shall remain in effect until changed or modified in accordance with Railway Labor Act, as amended.

[the agreement was signed by the General Chairman, Order of Railway Conductors and Brakemen; the Director of Labor Relations for the Chesapeake and Ohio Railway Company; and the Vice President, Order of Railway Conductors and Brakemen].

A separate agreement was signed between the C&O and the trainmen on the Northern Region (Pere Marquette District) and was effective March 27, 1968. There were minor differences between this agreement and the one reproduced above. The Northern Region agreement required that "rebuilt" or "new" pool cabooses be equipped with hand-operated windshield wipers. The sections relating to minerun cabooses was eliminated in the Northern Region agreement. An additional requirement of the Northern Region agreement was that brakemen would be held responsible for knowing that their cabs had been properly equipped with items required for flag protection.

[the Northern Region agreement was signed at Detroit,

Michigan, the 27th day of March, 1968, by the General Chairman, Brotherhood of Railroad Trainmen; the Vice President, Brotherhood of Railroad Trainmen; the C&O Director of Labor Relations for the Hocking Division; and the C&O Director of Labor Relations for the Northern Region (Pere Marquette District)].

As a follow-up to the pooling agreement documented above, which allowed pooling cabooses within a division, additional pooling which allowed cabs to continue with their train throughout the railroad and over different divisions was issued, at least at Columbus, Ohio, by a Superintendent's Bulletin dated March 30, 1982, and is reproduced here:

"Effective 0001, April 1, 1982, cabooses will be pooled in road freight service on the Columbus Subdivision (excluding the Columbus-Fostoria Straight-a-Way Local) and on the Athens Subdivision for crews with Columbus as home terminal, under provisions of the Caboose Pooling Agreement of March 27, 1968."

Other documentation on caboose pooling on the C&O indicated that cabooses would be pooled on or after 10-19-81 in Russell to Cincinnati service, but that the pooling could not be extended to Chicago because sufficient lockers were not available for the use of crews at Peru, Indiana, as required by the pooling agreement.

Phil Shuster comments: "It seemed that the incidents of fires in cabooses took a leap upward after the stoves were changed from coal to oil. The oil stoves were left burning almost continuously in cold weather while the coal stoves would burn out if left unattended. I can't imagine the need for two stoves. One would sweat you out in no time if set on high!"

Michigan winters are cold—cold enough that C&O officials experimented with 903152 by installing a stove in each end of the car, as can be seen by the two smoke jacks. This is the only caboose known to have received that interesting modification. Other railroads also have used two stoves in their cabooses. The 903152 was photographed on July 4, 1985, at Plymouth, Michigan. *Dwight Jones*

More on 903152's Two Stoves

Caboose 903152 was actually photographed (above) at Plymouth, Michigan (not Flint as incorrectly stated in the original edition of this book). The photo of this car originally appeared in the book to illustrate the fact that two stoves had been installed in this caboose. After publication official internal correspondence was discovered which provided details about this unusual installation.

In a February 4, 1976, memo, from the UTU C&O Local Chairman to the General Chairman, the complaint was lodged that C&O caboose 3152, in use on the Chicago Subdivision, on an assigned run, had one of three bunks missing due to installation of two new stoves—the installation of one of which necessitated the removal of a bunk. It was the Local Chairman's contention that this caboose was in violation of the caboose agreement which called for three bunks. It was further suggested that one of the remaining two bunks could be "double decked" to provide the required third bunk to satisfy the agreement requirements.

A handwritten note on the bottom of the memo indicated that the second stove had been installed around Christmas 1975.

A March 19, 1976, memo indicated that caboose 3152 was selected as an experiment for installing two stoves, one in each end.

One last memo, dated May 6, 1976, from the railroad's Labor Relations personnel to the UTU General Chairman indicated that an investigation revealed that the removal of the one bunk resulted from the installation of a second stove in caboose 3152 for experimental purposes and was based on a complaint made by the UTU General Chairman following a meeting in Baltimore on May 29, 1975.

Apparently the UTU complained about lack of heat so a second stove was installed for evaluation, at which time the UTU complained about the bunk removal.

One of the C&O's early wide-vision cabooses is shown at the International Car plant at Kenton, Ohio, as part of a long string of new cars undergoing final preparations for delivery. *C&O Historical Society Collection*

Still in original paint, 3181, with a "C" prefix to its number, crosses a trestle near Vinton, Ohio, on December 8, 1982, with a unit coal train bound for the Kyger Creek, Ohio, power plant. This train operated with a caboose at each end to reduce switching and was the last hurrah for this southeastern Ohio line. A bike path occupies most of the line these days. *Dwight Jones*

Elimination of duplicate equipment numbers was only one reason for renumbering caboose cars. Box 3322 carries the same road number as the premier Chessie caboose 3322. Locomotive numbers in the 3500 and 3300 series also conflicted with caboose numbers. The box car was a fixture at Columbus, Ohio, when photographed on October 31, 1982. *Dwight Jones*

Cupola Windshield Wipers

If one examines in-service photos of wide-vision cabooses it can be seen that some cars have cupola end windshield wipers and other cars do not. What gives? In order to examine this question we first checked specifications for these cabooses. The first 100 cars in series 3100-3199 were delivered without the windshield wipers. The balance of the cars, in series 3200-3325 were equipped with wipers "as built".

Next it appeared that many of those cars in series 3100-3199 were given wipers after delivery, but not all of them. Why were only some cars in this series given the wipers? A photo study shows that the cars that received the wipers after delivery were cars assigned to service in Michigan. As can be seen from the union agreement presented earlier in this chapter, it was a union requirement that pool cabooses used on the Pere Marquette District be equipped with the cupola windshield wipers. These wipers were operated manually so it was an easy retrofit, most likely completed at Grand Rapids.

A minor mishap damaged 3283, shown on June 5, 1977, at the Parsons Yard car shops, Columbus, Ohio. Repair work subsequently was performed at the Raceland car shops, and the cab was released back to service in February 1982 in Chessie yellow. (STD) *Dwight Jones*

(Below) C&O 903173 was involved in a wreck on Big Sandy that ended its productive days. It is shown loaded in a B&O gondola at the Russell car shops on June 21, 1986. The following month it was sold for scrap to Mansbach Metal of nearby Ashland, Kentucky. *Dwight Jones*

On July 26, 1981, a westbound coal train struck the rear of a stopped westbound coal train and then an eastbound empties train was involved as it rolled by at MR Cabin near Waverly, Ohio. Caboose 3221 is shown in this precarious position above the short hood of GP9 5927. Incredibly, no one was killed in this wreck which involved the derailment of three locomotives and 31 cars. C&O wreck crews from Columbus were dispatched to the site as were private contractors from Columbus and Blufton, Indiana. This heavily damaged caboose was repaired at Grand Rapids and emerged in Chessie yellow paint in November 1985.

Jim Henry Collection

It always was enjoyable to discover a C&O caboose which had been repainted into the Chessie scheme at the Raceland shops. One normally could find something "different" about the scheme. Add this car to that list. Apparently following the painting and lettering drawings was not a high priority at Raceland. Note the orange diagonal stripes on the end of the roof, replicating the yellow stripes on the original blue scheme. Interestingly this car arrived at the Raceland shops already in the Chessie scheme, having been painted at Grand Rapids in May 1977. The 903116 is shown at Russell, Kentucky, on June 16, 1985. *Dwight Jones*

The article at right appeared in a Columbus, Ohio, newspaper on September 2, 1968, announcing the new C&O wide-vision cabooses and featuring a photo of the 3111.

C&O Buys Cabooses

Chesapeake & Ohio Railway, as a first step in modernizing its caboose car fleet, is putting into service 100 new, modern cabooses which are a far cry from the old-time "crummies" (as they used to be called). These cabooses have extended cupolas for unrestricted observation and are equipped with electric lights, oil-burning heating stoves, cushion-type floating center sills with roller bearings, and aluminum window sashes. They also have flush-type toilets and refrigerators with water coolers, and are painted in "enchantment" blue with yellow reflective paint. The cabooses are being built for C&O by the International Car Co. in Kenton, O.

Active caboose service is over for 903242, photographed at Glenwood, Pennsylvania, on December 15, 1985. The excessively scorched side next to the caboose stove is an apparent indication of where this fire originated. *Dwight Jones*

76 Steel Cabooses of the Chesapeake & Ohio

The First Chessie Caboose

Chessie CEO Hays Watkins posed with an artists' rendition of what a Chessie-painted caboose would look like. The actual color artwork, above right, now is in the collection of the C&O Historical Society. Ironically, the actual 3238 never was repainted into the Chessie scheme and remains to this day in its original blue paint (see page 129).

C&O 3322 actually was the first caboose selected to be painted into the Chessie System scheme. The caboose was painted at the Huntington shops in September 1972. It then became a member of the special public relations display train that toured the railroad, being placed on display at key cities, including Pittsburgh, at left, on October 15, 1972, and at Baltimore, below, where after being displayed at the B&O Transportation Museum, the caboose and two freight cars were moved to this location near the U.S.S. Frigate *Constellation*, the first ship of the U.S. Navy, now permanently docked at Pier 1, Pratt Street. *Left: John C. LaRue, Jr, below: C&OHS collection*

(Above) Except for marker light replacement, 3322 was virtually unchanged and still wore the Huntington shops' 1972 yellow paint after ten years of service as the premier Chessie caboose. It was relegated to a less glamourous chore than display when photographed on October 10, 1982, in assigned service at Detroit's Rougemere Yard. (STD) *Dwight Jones*

C&O 903322 spent its last working days in local service out of the B&O yard at Brooklyn Junction, West Virginia. Needing mechanical repairs, it was dispatched to the Parkersburg, West Virginia, shops and from there it was placed into long term Heavy Bad Order storage in Parkersburg. It was shoved out of the way in the weeds on a stub end storage track. Vandals subsequently set the car on fire (some time prior to May 2008), destroying the interior. The two photos at left were taken on February 7, 2009. This cab was purchased in May 2009 by a private owner who planned to convert it to a bunk house on his farm. However, after being appraised of the car's history, he was rethinking those plans. *Dwight Jones*

This nonstandard paint/lettering scheme on C-3180 is believed to have been applied by the C&O car department forces at Silver Grove (Stevens Yard), Kentucky, in October 1978. It features smaller-than-specified lettering, no vermilion roof stripe, no blue cupola roof stripe, and other peculiarities. The interesting car was photographed at Silver Grove on May 4, 1980. *Dwight Jones*

Another interesting lettering variation is shown on this car. Someone apparently was just a little confused about how that ampersand should be applied (it is upside down on this car). The renumbering was accomplished at Port Huron, Michigan, on February 9, 1985. The car was photographed at St. Clair, Michigan, on July 5, 1985. *Dwight Jones*

C&O 3122 was only the fourth car from the wide-vision lot to be retired. It was involved in a System Accident at Newaygo, Michigan, on June 29, 1977. Thereafter it was dispatched in a gondola to the Russell shops for evaluation, and from there it was retired and sold to Portsmouth Iron & Metal, Portsmouth, Ohio, where it is shown on May 28, 1978. *Dwight Jones*

A common occurrence after the mid-1980s was the wholesale elimination and scrapping of the bulk of the C&O caboose fleet. C&O 903127 is suffering its fate at Columbus, Ohio, on August 9, 1992. Many cars were shipped off to scrap yards where they could be scrapped efficiently. Some cars had mechanical problems and could not travel on their own wheels and were sold for scrapping locally by roving scrap contractors, as was the case with this car. *Dwight Jones*

Photos on this page show interior furnishings of caboose 3260 when new at the International Car plant at Kenton, Ohio. The interiors were painted Vista Green. The butcher block type floors were very attractive when the cars were new. The photo at left shows the oil stove on the left and a bunk on the right.

This view shows the opposite end of the caboose. At left is a bunk with overhead water tank. A paper cup dispenser is mounted to the wall below the water tank. The ice box shows at the end of the bunk. On the right is another bunk with a padded fixed seat on this end of the bunk. A desk is in front of the seat.

Two photos courtesy CSX Mechanical Department

80 Steel Cabooses of the Chesapeake & Ohio

C&O caboose 903200 is shown on its side after being rear-ended by a following train that obviously had a difficult time stopping. Records indicated that the caboose was destroyed while operating on the Seaboard System at Dayton, Georgia. Subsequently it was retired by the Huntington Car Department on December 3, 1985. Sometimes it is difficult for a large railroad to keep track of all of its equipment, particularly when mergers are involved and different methods of equipment record histories on the component roads need to be combined by the new parent company. A November 2009 list of CSX cabooses that were in question was sent to the author by CSX for review and comment as to current status. This car, C&O 903200, was still being carried as active in those records. Its status now has been cleared up, as has the status of several dozen other cabs. *Lon Coone Photo, collection of Dwight Jones*

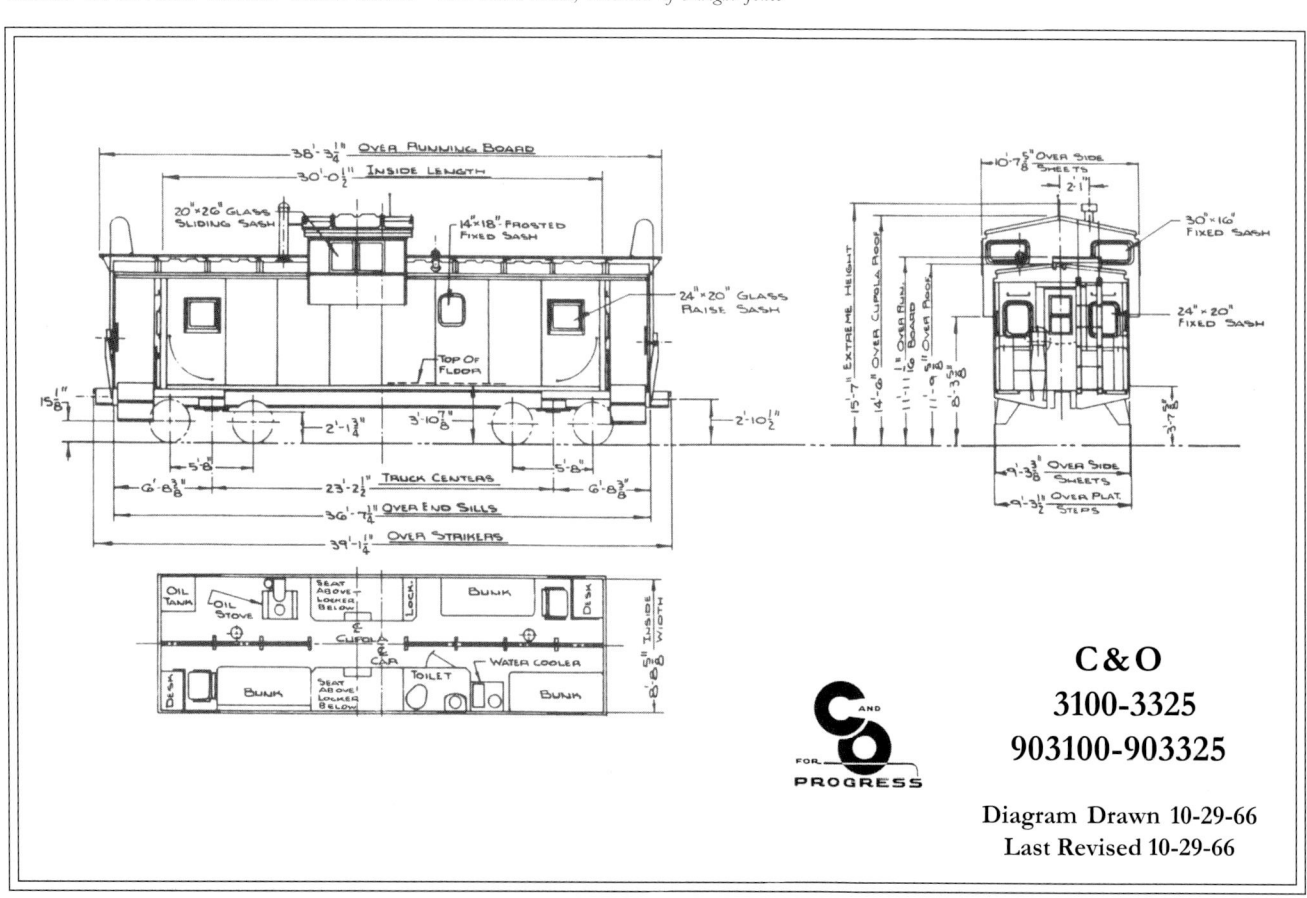

C&O
3100-3325
903100-903325

Diagram Drawn 10-29-66
Last Revised 10-29-66

Chapter 13

C&O 3500-3684 Series

One of the most ambitious caboose rebuilding programs in the history of the C&O took place in 1969 and 1970. Caboose cars 22 to 33 years old were routed from all parts of the system to the car shops at Grand Rapids, Michigan, where they were stripped to the shell and rebuilt.

Selected for the rebuilding program were cars from series 90000 to 90199—the oldest original C&O steel cabooses then on the roster. A total of 185 of these venerable veterans were rebuilt at Grand Rapids over a 21-month period in three different lots during 1969 and 1970.

Summary Table of Class C-15C Cabooses

SERIES	QTY.	Date Rebuilt	WEIGHT
3500-3574	75	1/69-5/69	47,500
3575-3624	50	9/69-12/69	47,500
3625-3684	60	5/70-9/70	47,500

The rebuilding program was not a simple matter of applying a few coats of paint and new road numbers. The participating cars were completely rebuilt inside and out. First, the cars were stripped to their shells. Windows, doors, window awnings, brake wheels and staffs, and all interior fittings were removed—even the interior walls and ceilings were torn out. The remaining car shell then was sandblasted to remove all paint and rust.

Next, the cars progressed in assembly-line fashion through the old Grand Rapids shop building, where all-new windows and doors were applied, a new roof was added over the old one, and new roller-bearing trucks were placed under the cars. New plywood interior walls and ceilings were installed, and new oil heaters and other interior fittings were added.

The cars were finished with a fresh coat of the six-month-old blue paint scheme that made its debut on the 3100-series cabooses. The rebuilt cars also were assigned new four-digit road numbers in the combined C&O/B&O caboose numbering system. The new numbers began at 3500 (probably to allow for future acquisition of wide-vision cupola cars, if more cabooses were needed).

When completed, the 3500-3684 series cabooses, along with new wide-vision cupola cabooses, formed the backbone of the C&O caboose fleet, and both types of cars could be found operating all across mainline territory. At that time, all first-line C&O cabooses were in the blue paint scheme. In fact, in 1971 blue cabooses accounted for just about exactly half of the entire C&O caboose fleet. Secondary cabooses remained in the yellow scheme and were used mostly in yard, transfer, mine, and branch-line service.

C&O 3675 is shown on April 22, 1975, at Alma, Michigan. *John C. LaRue Collection*

The following photos document the extensive rebuilding program carried out at the C&O's Grand Rapids car shops. The photos originally were shot by the C&O Public Relations Department and are from the collection of the C&O Historical Society. All were taken around January 1969.

Cabooses 90060 and 90183 are shown beginning their conversion at Grand Rapids in the photo above. Everything is stripped from the interior of these first-generation cabooses and is thrown outside to be cleaned up by this small bulldozer. In Michigan, your bulldozer needs an all-weather cab! Not only are the interior fittings removed, but, as the photo below shows, original tongue-and-groove sheathing is cut up and thrown away to be replaced with plywood. After being stripped, the remaining caboose "shell" is moved to the blast area where old paint and body rust is removed. Note that this older first-generation steel cab had been upgraded to have a long, permanently attached angle cock handle which runs up along the left side of the end ladder.

83

Above left: Inside the Grand Rapids shops, new roller-bearing trucks have been assembled and are about to be rolled under the car in the background. Note the generator unit mounted to the end of the axle. Above right: a shop worker uses an air nailer to apply new plywood sheathing to the walls. Below: New windows, roof, and running boards have been installed on these cars. A welder in the background appears to be working around the side window.

84   Steel Cabooses of the Chesapeake & Ohio

A comparison of before and after views documents the extent of the interior refurbishment. The new interiors were painted Vista Green. Floors were painted brown and interior handholds were black. The view at top right shows an electric ceiling light, new oil stove and padded corners for safety. The fuel tank shows in the photo at bottom left.

When finished, they looked like this. C&O 3522 is virtually an entirely new caboose. Roofs were originally specified to be painted light gray. Only early cars received the gray roofs. Blue was specified after the first few cars were completed. We believe the early cars had their roofs repainted blue before release to service.[11]

Shown at the Grand Rapids shops on October 9, 1982, C3626 was the last surviving car of the class still in blue paint. Already the old lettering stickers have been burned off and new marker lights and **FRA** windows have been installed. The car is almost ready to receive yellow paint and Chessie System lettering. It was outshopped from Grand Rapids in October 1982. *Dwight Jones*

A hot day at Charlottesville, Virginia, on August 1, 1982, found 903679 holding down a spot on the cab track. The local Trainmaster apologized for the condition of "his" cabooses. "We've ordered brushes and cleaning supplies from Clifton Forge. Couldn't you come to photograph them after they've been washed?" Some C-15/C-15c cabooses have metal plates welded to the left of the door to seal old window openings. This car doesn't.[12] The new six digit number applied above the end window makes this a non-standard lettering scheme. *Dwight Jones*

Ladders and Running Boards

As was the case with the wide-vision cabooses, running boards and end ladders were a part of the original specifications for these cars. An analysis of photos shows that cars 3500-3624 had them while subsequent cabooses in this rebuilt group did not. Some of these first cars later had their running boards and end ladders removed. When that happened a large stencil was applied to the outside near the steps indicating that—most likely to notify crews who were familiar with equipment on a specific caboose number.

C&O 903530 is in fresh paint at Russell on May 29, 1982. This car was painted at Grand Rapids the previous month and shows the typical Chessie System paint scheme for these cars with one exception—the approved scheme should have the C&O reporting marks stacked over the road number. The small lettering under the number indicates the car has been equipped with **FRA** window glazing. *Dwight Jones*

86   Steel Cabooses of the Chesapeake & Ohio

Painting and lettering deviations that result in unorthodox schemes are interesting and offer relief from the "fleet appearance". Seldom are such lettering variations as drastic as observed here on the 903651, shown at Russell on November 24, 1983. Painted in September 1983, this cupola caboose was given "Chessie System" lettering normally applied to a bay-window caboose! It's no surprise to learn this car was painted at Raceland. *Dwight Jones*

Two more interesting lettering variations are shown by these two cabooses. Chessie's safety emblem was standard attire on the road's 23 multicolored safety cabooses, and on class C-27 and C-27A bay-window cabooses. Other older cabooses did not get the emblems—except, that is, for some assigned to St. Albans and Danville, West Virginia. Almost all of the locally assigned cabooses at St. Albans had small safety emblems such as the one worn by 3668, photographed at St. Albans on July 31, 1982. Similar St. Albans applications appeared on 90328, 903647, 90286, 90304 and 900219. Only the 903586, which was assigned to Danville, received a much larger emblem—most likely of the same size as applied to the new bay-window cabooses built at FGE. The 903586 was photographed at the Raceland car shops on June 16, 1985, where it was held for repairs. *both, Dwight Jones*

87

Just as builders' photos give an idea of a car's appearance when it joined the roster, the photos on this page present to readers an idea of how, and why, cars leave the roster. At Cincinnati on March 3, 1984, 903595 showed little physical damage while riding on a white-lined Western Maryland flat.

C&O 903637 had extensive body damage to both ends when it was photographed at the Russell car shops on December 23, 1984. It was sold two months later to scrap dealer Mansbach Metal. *both photos, Dwight Jones*

When cars cannot move on their own wheels, a contract scrap crew must be dispatched to the location of the cars that are to be scrapped. In this photo, at Columbus, Ohio, on May 23, 1982, C&O 903564 is being loaded, panel by panel, into a truck to be hauled back to a scrap yard. Prior to being loaded the car was set on fire to remove all wood and other burnable items. *Dwight Jones*

88   Steel Cabooses of the Chesapeake & Ohio

About three dozen cabooses were present, and "C" prefix road numbers were the norm when this September 7, 1980, photo was made at the Russell cab track. A large number of the cabooses in this photo were rebuilt 3500 and 3600 series cars. One can imagine that it was quite a job to keep all of these cabooses serviced. *Dwight Jones*

Cupola Windshield Wipers

As was the case with the wide vision cabooses, select cars in the 3500-3684 series were equipped with windshield wipers. As was stated in the previous chapter, this was a union requirement for cabooses operating on the Pere Marquette District (Michigan and Canada).

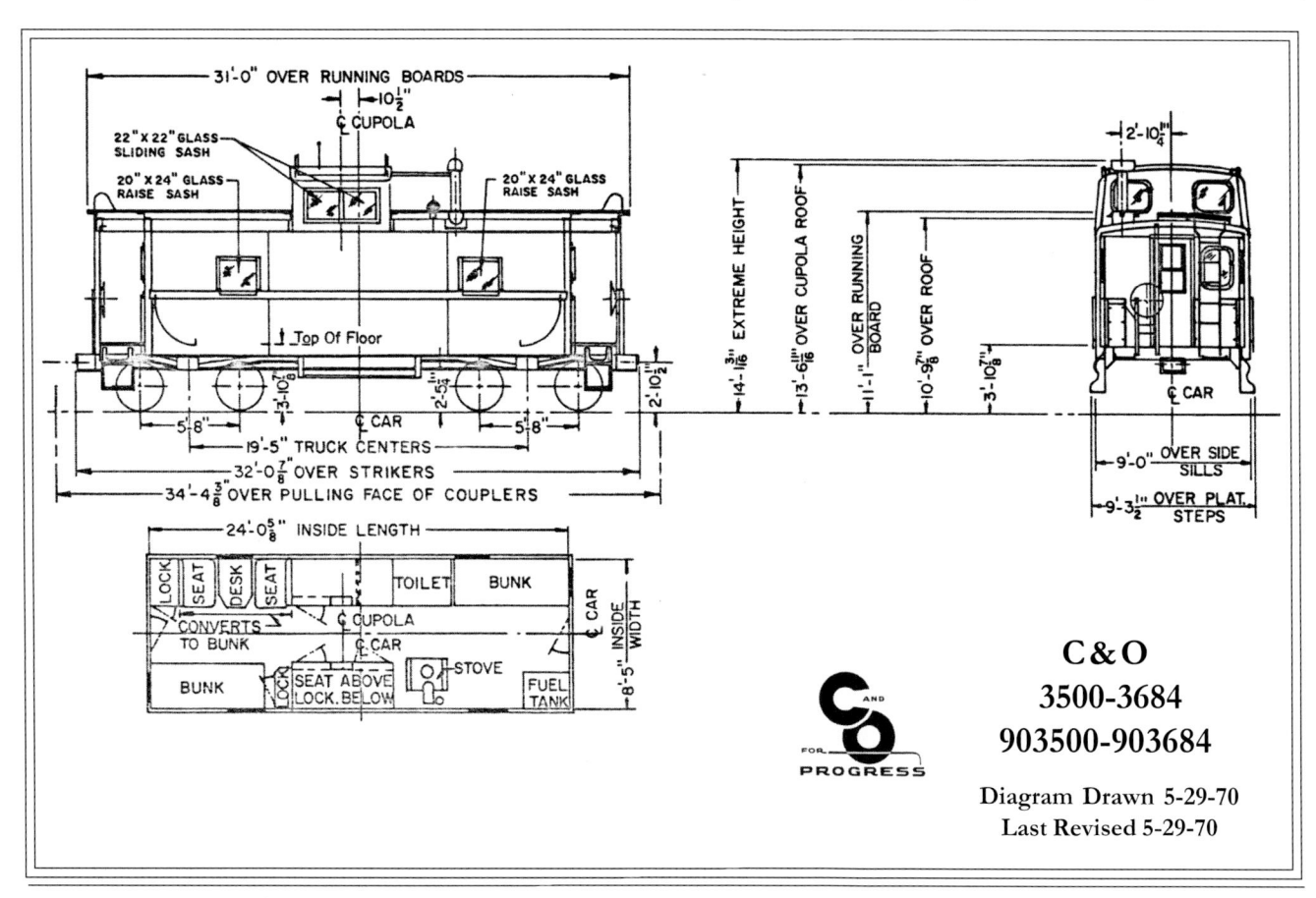

C&O
3500-3684
903500-903684

Diagram Drawn 5-29-70
Last Revised 5-29-70

Chapter 14

C&O 904094-904159 Series

The year 1980 marked the end of a long drought for the acquisition of new cabooses by the C&O. It had been nearly a decade since the last cars of the C-25 class were delivered by International Car in 1971. Well over 250 cabooses, about 30 percent of the 1971 roster total, had been removed from service during the 1970s. The few wood-sheathed cabs remaining in service were on their last legs and needed to be replaced. The time was right for new cabooses.

Although no C&O cabooses had been purchased since 1971, the ranks of the Chessie cab fleet had continued to grow with the addition of new B&O cars.

B&O Cabooses Acquired in the 1970s

    128 cabooses purchased in 1970-71
     97 cabooses purchased in 1975
     62 cabooses purchased in 1978
    ―――
    287 Total

It was not a surprise, therefore, when the announcement was made that new C&O cabooses would be acquired in the early 1980s. What was a shock was the fact that the cars would be of the standard B&O bay-window design—never before used on C&O. The 160-car order, placed with Fruit Growers Express of Alexandria, Virginia, was divided between both B&O and C&O.

Who Got What in 1980:
    B&O 904000-904093, 94 cars
    C&O 904094-904159, 66 cars

Although the lower road numbers were assigned to the B&O cars, it was the C&O cars that were built first at the request of the Transportation Department due to a critical need for cabooses on C&O lines. The premier car, C&O 904094, was rushed to completion in order to participate in a special display train for the 1980 stockholder's meeting held at then-new Queensgate Yard in Cincinnati. After display at Cincinnati the car was billed to the Grand Rapids shops to be outfitted for service. It was during this trip that the car received the dubious honor of being the first car of the class to be derailed—and it hadn't even made it into active service yet! Damage was only minor, and the car soon was put into use on

First of 160 class C-27A cabooses and first-ever C&O baywindow caboose was "C"4094. The road number was changed to 904094 before release from the FGE plant (STD). *C&O Railway*

the Michigan Division until being reassigned to Richmond, Virginia, at a later date.

The rest of the C&O cars started appearing about a month after the first car. Released from the FGE plant more or less weekly in groups of two or three, the cars were routed through Clifton Forge, Russell, and Toledo to their destination of Grand Rapids, where they were outfitted for service. All 66 cars made their home, at least initially, on the Michigan Division, most running out of Grand Rapids.

The C-27A cars' presence in Michigan permitted the reassignment of many older steel cupola cabooses to other divisions, which, in turn, allowed for the quick retirement of the few remaining wood-sheathed cabooses.

As time went by a few of the cars were "loaned" to other regions of the C&O, and by mid-1983 the following cars had been stationed at other locales:
904094-904098 loaned to Richmond, Virginia
904143, 904145 loaned to Hinton, West Virginia

A number of B&O cabooses from the C-27A class were likewise sent to the C&O at Hinton for use on coal trains between Hinton and Clifton Forge—the philosophy apparently being that these new cabooses could better withstand the rigors of heavy-duty pusher service over the Allegheny Mountains. The B&O cabs assigned to Hinton were in the series 904080 to 904093. All were returned to B&O lines when pooling of C&O cabooses was implemented on the Virginia and West Virginia Divisions.

By 1984 the majority of the C&O bay-window cabooses had filtered off the Michigan Division and could be found in general pool service across both the C&O and B&O as the railroad worked to gradually implement a system-wide C&O/B&O/WM caboose pool.

An FGE ad in *Railway Age* featured a color photo of C&O C4094 along with Southern X315 and L&N 6600.

Caboose "C"4094 became "90"4094 before release from the FGE plant, and therefore has the distinction of being the first Chessie caboose renumbered to the six-digit road number series. Rushed to completion for a stockholders meeting display at Cincinnati's Queensgate yard, the car had to have the safety emblem painted on the sides, as on the previous order of B&O C-27 cabooses. Reflectorized decal stickers arrived later and were used on the rest of the order. Shown at Walbridge, Ohio, on September 4, 1980, the car had been in service just five short months. (STD)

Dwight Jones

Above, by the date of the author's visit to the FGE shops, on September 18, 1980, the C&O cars already had been completed and released to service. But cars for the B&O still were in the process of being constructed. Here a group progresses down the assembly line. *Dwight Jones*

An end view shows the first C-27A caboose at FGE's plant. Cars were wired to receive backup lights later, if needed, as evidenced by the offset FRA light and external plug to the left. Three swatches of red reflectorized material were applied to the ends, one on either side of the door behind the upper grabirons, and another just to the right of the brake wheel. A "T" handle extension allowed employees standing on the end platform an easy way to turn the angle cock. As noted earlier, this first car was renumbered to 904094 before release from the FGE shops. The opposite end of the car did not have an end window. (STD) *C&O Railway*

When new, the **C&O** C-27A cabooses were sent across the **C&O** system to Russell in groups of two or three as they made their way to their new assignments in Michigan. Here three of the new cars are caught enroute at Russell, Kentucky, on June 29, 1980. *Dwight Jones*

Above, C&O 3210 seems strangely out of place with this string of new C-27A bay-window cars at Hinton, West Virginia, on April 24, 1982. These **B&O** bay-window cars were sent to the area to be used on trains requiring pusher assists between Hinton and Clifton Forge. *Dwight Jones*

What an interesting photo this turned out to be of an eastbound train at White Sulphur Tunnel on July 30, 1983, with 904143. There were only seven C&O C-27A cabs assigned to the Virginia Division at this date, the two helper units were both Western Maryland, they were consecutively numbered (7571, 7570) and they both were still in WM black paint! *Dwight Jones*

93

Several different styles of stenciling road numbers are shown on these cabooses, on the Mosel Yard cab track at Columbus, Ohio, on April 30, 1983. Sometimes shops like to "wing it" or perhaps they received a special request from Transportation officers. It appears that the last four digits of the road number was painted on the bay ends of all or most of the bay-window cars at the Grand Rapids shops after delivery. This application was unique to the C&O C-27A cars. Behind the 904122 is the 3656, which has been given a "90" number on its sides, but retains the previous "C" prefix number on the ends of its cupola. *Dwight Jones*

Above, this overhead view of 904101 at Walbridge, Ohio, on July 2, 1982, shows the simplified uncluttered roof and the steel grating used in construction of the steps and end platforms. The vertical application of the last four road number digits to the bay ends also shows on this car. *Dwight Jones*

An in-service casualty was 904140, shown at B&O's Barr Yard car shops in Chicago on September 1, 1984. Moved to Russell, Kentucky, for storage at a later date, this car became the first of the C-27A class to be officially retired. It was retired at Russell on December 3, 1986. It was sold as scrap about two years later, in November 1988, to scrap dealer Mansbach Metal of Ashland, Kentucky. Virtually all cars written up as scrap at Russell would meet their fate at nearby Mansbach. *Dwight Jones*

94   Steel Cabooses of the Chesapeake & Ohio

two photos, Dwight Jones

In 1986 six C&O bay-window cabooses were given a blue swatch on their bay sides, beneath the road numbers, and special lettering was applied indicating the cars were in assigned international service. The specially stencilled cars operated between Detroit and Buffalo through the Province of Ontario, Canada. The cabs received the markings because they were outfitted with special radios to allow crews to communicate with any railroad that they operated on while traveling between Detroit and Buffalo. Different frequencies were needed to talk with CSX at Detroit, Conrail at Detroit, CN and CP through Canada, Conrail at Buffalo (which was different than Conrail at Detroit) and B&O at Buffalo (which used a different frequency than CSX in Detroit). As of early 1987, end-of-train devices were restricted in Canada, and all CSX trains operating in that country were running with cabooses. However, Canadian hearings were proceeding, and CSX anticipated operating without cabooses possibly as early as mid-1987. At that time, the special radios likely would be assigned to certain locomotives. The two photos on this page were taken at C&O's Rougemere Yard in Detroit. On January 24, 1987, the following was the status of the six international cabooses:

904109 at Detroit
904111 shopped at Detroit
904117 en route: Detroit to Buffalo
904121 at Fargo, Ontario
904125 at Buffalo
904156 at Buffalo

C&O 904131, assigned at Columbus, Ohio, developed center sill problems that prevented moving the car on its own wheels. Typically such a car would be scrapped on site. Sometimes the cost of loading a car and moving it to a shop is justified. On August 8, 2002, contractors were loading 904131 on a specially equipped flat to ship the car to the system caboose shop at Jacksonville. CSX uses a number of these 89-foot flat cars which are equipped with adjustable bolster adaptors, that will accept any length of car, and which have special pockets to hold trucks on the end. The flats are painted red and are numbered in the 600,000 series. The 904131 was repaired and was released as CSXT shoving platform 900070 without repainting. The solar equipment (see page 121) was removed while the car was at the shop. *Dwight Jones*

Not all cabooses were as fortunate as the 904131 pictured at the top of the page. This photo shows what happened to the 904097, being scrapped at Columbus on May 2, 1994. The body was cut away from the underframe and then was rolled over onto the roof. By 1999 nearly half of the C&O C-27A cars were gone from the roster. *Dwight Jones*

96 Steel Cabooses of the Chesapeake & Ohio

After completing the repainting of two cabooses in the Russell yard, 3191 for display at Russell and C3808 for shipment to the B&O Railroad Museum, Russell Terminal Manager Barry Totty requested that the author apply the C&O Business Unit logo to caboose 904128, which at that time was the only caboose operating out of Russell. It was assigned to the Vanceburg Turn. The original plan was to repaint the whole caboose, but it was wrecked not long after this October 9, 1994, photo was taken. The car subsequently was scrapped in June 1999. *Dwight Jones*

From the "what if" department. What if the C&O had retained their red caboose scheme and the original steam era "for Progress" emblem? The author couldn't resist fun with a little paint and stencils on this C-27A caboose shown at Columbus on July 11, 2004. *Dwight Jones*

A weather beaten 904157 still retaining original paint and C&O markings after 30 years of service is shown on the Huntington, West Virginia, rip track on May 15, 2010. The car had been recalled from Danville, West Virginia, to serve as the shoving platform for Huntington. It was being "fixed up" for that service on this date. Safety appliances had been given a fresh coat of white and yellow reflective strips have been applied along the sides. The car number also had been renewed on the roof ends. *Dwight Jones*

C&O 900034, photographed on November 19, 2008, is somewhat of an anomaly. Technically there is no such car. How can that be? At one time most yards had various "shacks" where yard workers could get in out of the rain, or get warmed on a cold winter day. Modernizations eliminated such "conveniences". Officers at Russell, Kentucky, set about to correct that injustice by coming up with the idea of placing a caboose in the middle of the yard as a shelter. The scheme selected for the caboose paid tribute to the heritage of the C&O and that of the Chessie System. A car was available which was stored in bad order at Russell, CSXT 900034 which was wearing the "Cross Tracks Safely" CSX scheme. The cab was moved to the Raceland car shops where it was repainted, being outshopped in January 2006. It was a good likeness of the original Chessie scheme. The graphics were stick-on type and the top and bottom side stripes were more red than Chessie vermilion, but the car did look good. For the trivia buffs—this was the last caboose painted at Raceland before the shops were taken over by a contract company. So why did we say there is technically no such caboose as C&O 900034? This car originally was B&O 904038! *Dwight Jones*

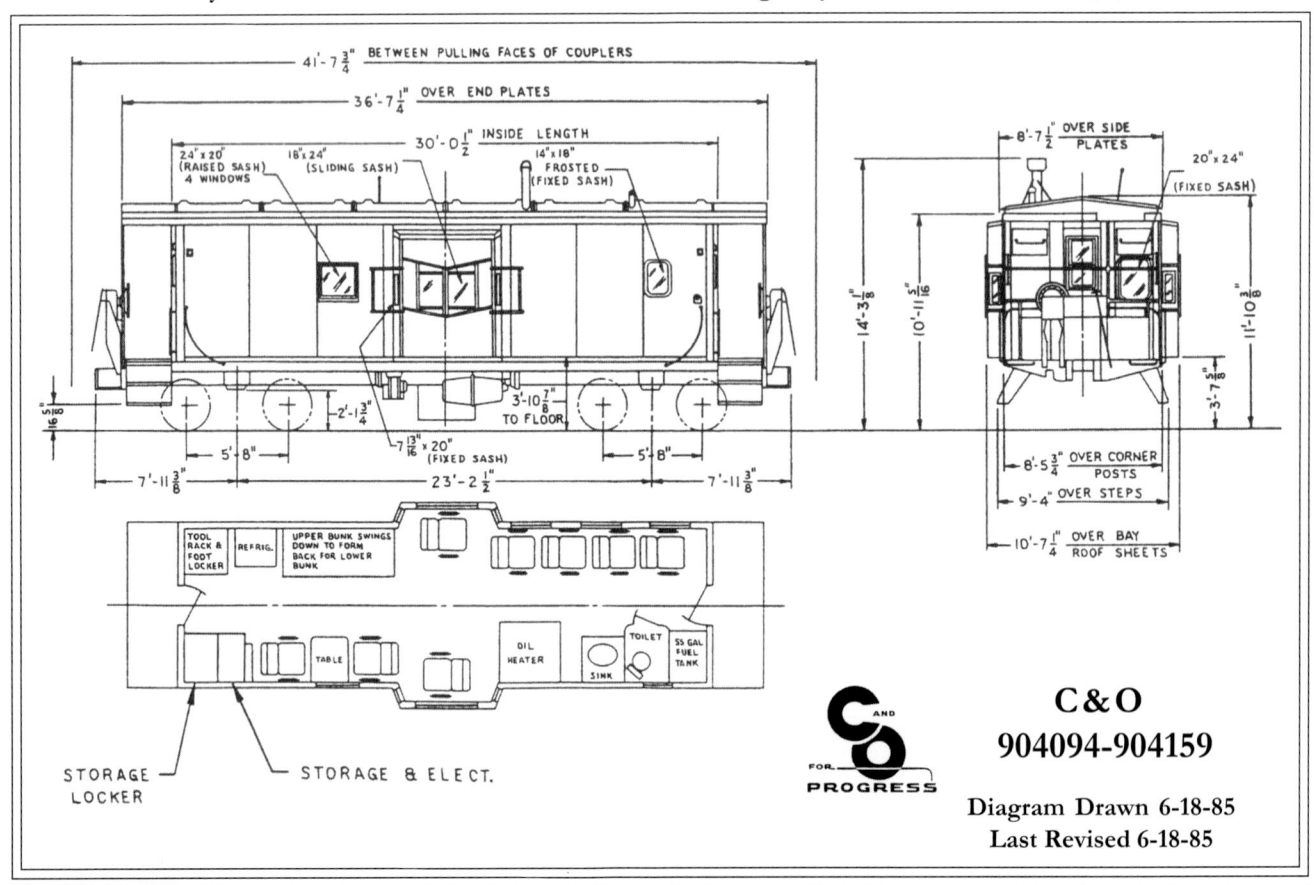

C&O
904094-904159

Diagram Drawn 6-18-85
Last Revised 6-18-85

98 Steel Cabooses of the Chesapeake & Ohio

Chapter 15

Toledo Terminal Cabs

On January 1, 1984, the Chesapeake & Ohio acquired the properties of the Toledo Terminal Railroad. The 28.59-mile line was formerly owned by four railroads—B&O (17.85 percent), C&O (28.56 percent), Conrail (42.87 percent), and Norfolk and Western (10.72 percent)—and served 26 shippers in its beltline operation around the city of Toledo.

Operating control was taken by C&O on July 1, 1984, and with that move the C&O had acquired four "new" cabooses and an assortment of other equipment. Toledo Terminal locomotives were replaced by Chessie geeps; TT track equipment was sent to Russell, Kentucky; and in December 1984 two of TT's four cabooses were moved to the C&O car shops at Walbridge for renumbering and restencilling for the new owner. A November 28, 1984, letter from Mechanical Department headquarters at Huntington gave instructions to the Walbridge car shops. "All references to the Toledo Terminal Railroad including car number and logos are to be painted out."

Toledo Terminal's red paint was retained in the makeshift relettering, which consisted only of painting over the old caboose number and railroad name and applying new C&O numbers and reporting marks in white. In early 1985 TT's other two cabooses received similar treatment. One could now say that the C&O owned honest-to-goodness "red" cabooses (of course, to be accurate, C&O also rostered one red "safety" caboose, C&O 3282 on the Ohio Division).

Toledo Terminal caboose #90 was of the Reading style and had been acquired secondhand. It originally had been built by Lehigh Valley. Cabooses 91-93, also acquired secondhand, were of the style manufactured by International Car in the late 1940s and early 1950s. Cars of this latter design were also owned by P&WV; GTW; DT&I; Roscoe, Snyder & Pacific; D&TSL; and Louisiana & North West.

It is interesting to note that road numbers 900357-900360 would have fit into the C&O caboose roster better than the road numbers actually assigned, particularly when one considers that caboose number 90 was of the same design as C&O series 900350-900356, which originally had been built by the Western Maryland.

C&O/Toledo Terminal caboose transfers predated this 1984 acquisition by three decades. In 1953 and 1955 Toledo Terminal acquired 12 secondhand wood-sheathed cabooses from C&O. They were assigned TT road numbers 170-181. The 12 former C&O cabooses came from series 90695-90886. The last car, number 175, was retired in 1978.[13]

The four steel former Toledo Terminal cabooses continued to call Toledo home until late 1986, when 903328 was sent to Russell, where it remained in January 1987.

Caboose 903327 displays the simplified lettering style applied by the shops at Walbridge to the former Toledo Terminal cabooses. The car is shown on February 23, 1985, at the former TT yard in Toledo. *Dwight Jones*

Toledo Terminal caboose 93 was one of three cabs of this standard International Car design which was extensively rebuilt for service on the TT by ICC. The three cars originally were Detroit & Toledo Shore Line cabooses. TT 93 was photographed at Toledo on July 2, 1982, painted caboose red with white lettering. *Dwight Jones*

C&O 903329 shows off its new lettering at Toledo on December 29, 1984, at the former TT yard. Three of the four TT cabooses were saved by private owners, including this car, former TT 93. *Dwight Jones*

Recently renumbered 903328 shares yard space with yellow C&O 900305 at the former Toledo Terminal yard in northern Toledo on February 23, 1985. *Dwight Jones*

Steel Cabooses of the Chesapeake & Ohio

An oddball on the Toledo Terminal roster was caboose 90, acquired directly from geographic neighbor Detroit & Toledo Shore Line. The cab originally was built by the Lehigh Valley. The car reportedly was in bad order storage when photographed on December 29, 1984. Its caboose days were over. *Dwight Jones*

TT 90 was renumbered to C&O 903326 on January 3, 1985, and appears not to have moved one inch from the date of the photo above. This photo was taken on February 23, 1985, at the TT shop in northern Toledo. The brick building in the background prevented taking a photo of the opposite side of the caboose. *Dwight Jones*

The date now is September 14, 1991, and the brick shop building has been demolished permitting a photo of the opposite side of the caboose, which reveals that the first digit of the new C&O number was applied upside down on this side, making the number 603326! This car was later sold to a private owner in Kentucky, who never picked it up. It then was sold to another private owner who has it displayed in his yard at **Walbridge**. *Dwight Jones*

101

When cabooses were removed from service, surplus cars were accumulated at select system locations. Many accumulated at Columbus, Ohio, including this former Toledo Terminal caboose, renumbered as 903329. For the July 1993 C&O Historical Society Conference, it was selected for a part of the equipment display at Parsons Yard. The author applied, to one side, the first generation "for Progress" emblem to add a little additional C&O flavor. The car is shown in Columbus on July 23, 1993. Trivia question: Was there a red caboose with first generation emblem on the railroad in 1993? Second trivia question: What was the last caboose to be acquired by the C&O? Answer to both: this car. *Dwight Jones*

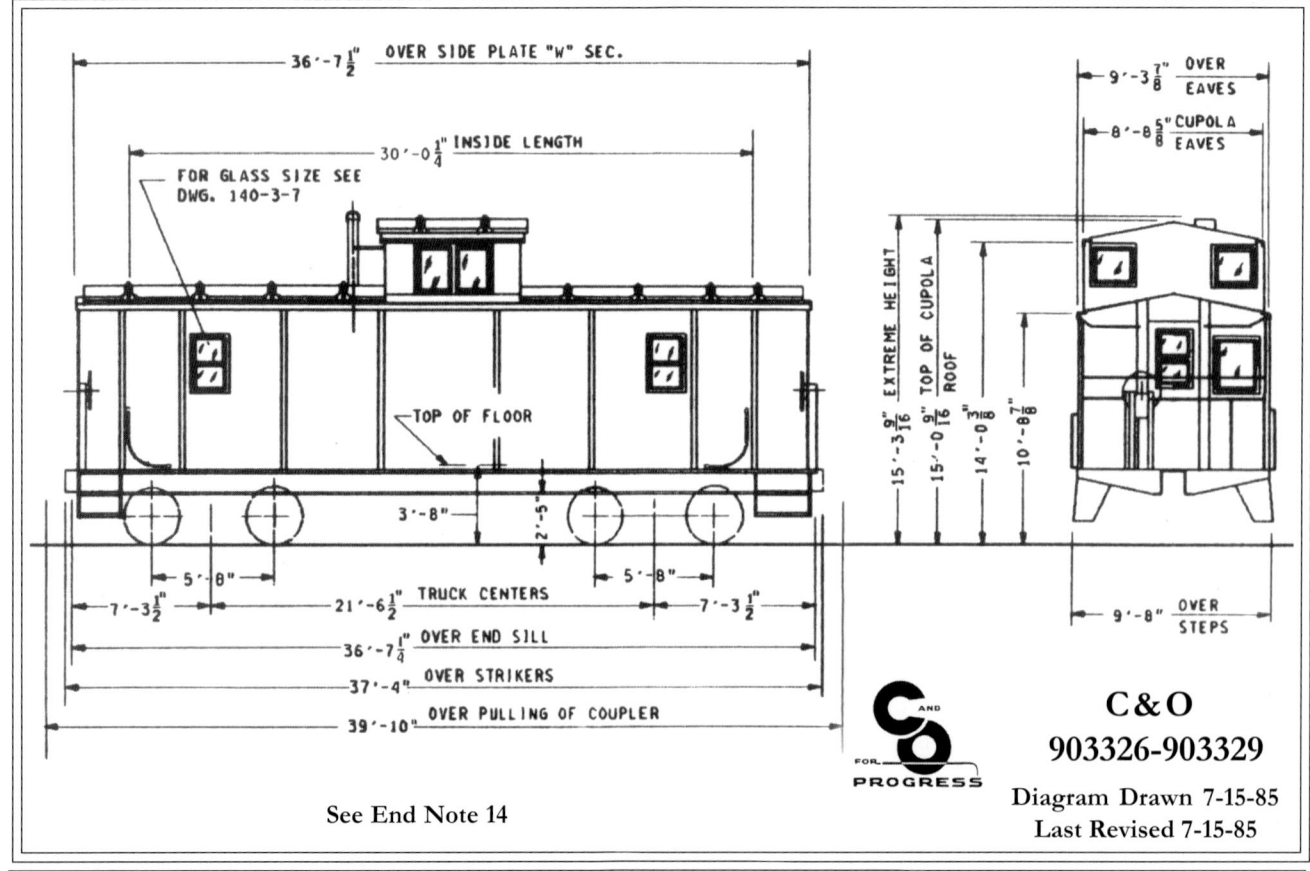

C&O 903326-903329

Diagram Drawn 7-15-85
Last Revised 7-15-85

See End Note 14

102   Steel Cabooses of the Chesapeake & Ohio

Toledo Terminal Caboose Lettering

Long time C&O Historian and former C&O employee Phil Shuster provides a most interesting account of the creation of the lettering scheme for the Toledo Terminal cabooses. Phil picks up his story below:

"On July 1, 1969, I left the Chesapeake & Ohio and accepted a position of Chief Engineer of the Toledo Terminal Railroad where I remained until the C&O takeover of that road in 1984.

"On a small railroad (six officers), everyone wears many (and each other's) hats, and often does jobs not normally associated with a title or position. One instance of this occurred at about 4:00 P.M. on Friday, July 12, 1974, when our President and General Manager came bursting into my office proclaiming, "International Car just called and they've got to have full size drawings of the lettering we want on the three "new" cabooses first thing Monday morning. O.K. (thanks for the long lead time, boss). He then proceeded to tell me that he wanted "Toledo Terminal" along the top just below the eaves, "sorta like on a passenger car letterboard", the Toledo Terminal Railroad diamond herald centered on the car body, and a large number ("so you can see it from a distance") centered toward the bottom. All of the small, car specification lettering would be taken care of by International Car. We had large (1 1/2" scale) general arrangement drawings of the cabooses and I was told to prepare what I thought would look good, given the above parameters, in layout on these drawings and let him see it before finalizing them. I called my wife to say I'd be late again, cleared off the old drafting table and plunged into caboose lettering. I had previously decalled a few O-scale cabooses, but this was for real.

"I've always been inclined toward Railroad Roman as a lettering style, but quickly decided that I didn't have enough time to play with all those curves and twists. It was going to have to be big, bold block letters produced by a straight edge and compass. I finished the layout by about 8:00 P.M. and called the boss who said he'd meet me at 7:00 A.M. to go over it. We met, he enthusiastically endorsed what I'd prepared, and I set out drawing the full-size (8") lettering and 12" numerals. We had several sizes of the diamond herald stencils (made from brass) on hand in the shop and we loaned one of these stencils to I.C.C. so I didn't have to make a drawing of that.

"At 8:00 A.M. on Monday I was at the Toledo Blueprint & Supply Company having prints made from my tracings and by 8:30 the prints were on their way to Kenton, Ohio, 1-1/2 hours away. Deadline met, and everyone (except my wife) was happy. A couple of weeks later the T&OC delivered three new (actually rebuilt, but looking and smelling like new) cabooses to the Toledo Terminal Railroad's Walbridge yard. I always thought they looked pretty darned good, and was proud of the small bit I had to play in their development."

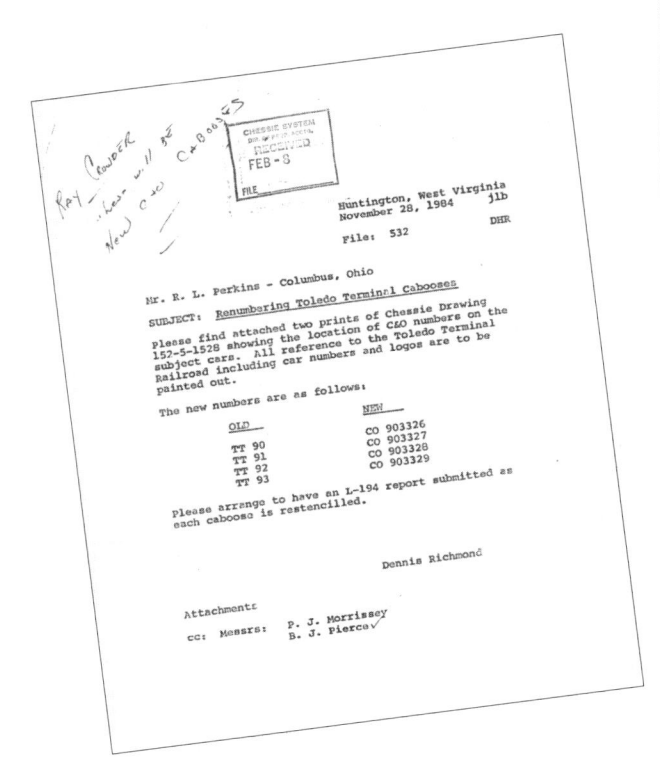

The Toledo Terminal Railroad also rostered a number of former C&O wood cupola cabooses, some of which the TT removed the cupolas from. More information on those cabooses can be found in the publication *Chesapeake and Ohio Cabooses, 90700 Series*, listed on page 144 in this publication.

Instructions to the field for work to be carried out was handled many times by the issuance of a standard memo. In the example at left, Mechanical Department officials at the OH Building in Huntington were instructing officers on the Ohio Division in regard to the relettering of the Toledo Terminal steel cabooses. *collection of Dwight Jones*

Toledo Terminal Caboose 91
Saved by the Author

Although we have long had an interest in caboose history, we never considered caboose ownership. One reason was we had no place to keep one. But in 1995 a seed was planted.

As cabooses were eliminated from through freights, the surplus cars were accumulated at select system locations. One of those locations was Columbus, Ohio, where a long line of out-of-service cabooses accumulated. One by one the cars with roller bearings were sold off or moved to shops for conversion to shoving platforms. Left behind were those cars which had friction bearings, which CSX would not allow to move over the railroad. Those cars would either have to be trucked out of Parsons by private owners, or would be sold to a scrap company that would cut them up at Parsons.

Another option opened up in 1995. CSX officials in Jacksonville had scheduled a routine audit of Parsons Yard, and there was a massive effort to get everything cleaned up and in order prior to that event. The CSX department responsible for disposing of obsolete assets was panicking—what to do with those 12 friction-bearing cabooses left at Parsons. They had to be removed from the property, and fast!

John Riddle had just retired from CSX as Ohio Division Superintendent of Operations at Parsons, and had become active on the Hocking Valley Scenic Railway at Nelsonville. CSX contacted John about the caboose dilemma. "Would the Hocking Valley be interested in all 12 cabooses at an attractive price? We need to get them off the property, all of them, quickly. If you would take all 12 of them you can have them for $300 each!"

Long story short, of course they would. John made the deal, and the cars quickly were moved into the carshop area to be serviced before being routed down the old Hocking line to Nelsonville. The plan developed by the HVSR board was that the cars would be offered for sale to members of the scenic line for the same $300, if they agreed to fix up the cabooses. There was no restriction on them keeping the cars on the HVSR but it was expected that most would.

On July 23, 1993, we spotted John's pickup truck in the Parsons carshop with the string of cabs. John was checking out the caboose that he had selected for himself, C&O 90211. We stopped in to talk with John. It did not take him long to begin the sales talk. "Dwight, why don't you join the Hocking Valley Scenic, then you can select one of these cabooses as yours, and fix it up!"

We thought about John's offer for a couple of days, and we were hooked. We called him back and asked about the availability of the other C&O caboose, 90221. It's already spoken for, John told us. OK, how about the former Toledo Terminal caboose, now C&O 903329. Also spoken for, John said. Those were the only cars in the string we were interested in. The remainder were of Clinchfield, L&N or SBD heritage. So much for that plan.

We continued to think about John's offer, and think just how good that Toledo Terminal caboose would look painted as a DT&I caboose. DT&I was one of our favorite roads and the body style of the TT cab was the same as cabooses used on the DT&I. Both roads had purchased cabs from International Car of Kenton, Ohio. The more we thought about it the more we were disappointed that the TT caboose had already been spoken for by one of the Hocking Valley Scenic officials.

On February 26, 1995, a total of 18 cabooses was lined up in storage at Columbus. The friction-bearing cabooses in this line would be headed for the Hocking Valley Scenic Railway in a few months. *Dwight Jones*

But wait a minute. There still was one of the TT cabs left at Walbridge yard in Toledo, and we suspected it was not in use. Some calls were made, and we were able to confirm that the car was stored. A call to Jacksonville provided this response: "Yes, Dwight, we can sell that car to you; price is $1200!" "Hey wait a minute—you just sold the sister car at Columbus not that long ago for $300!" Long pause on the phone, then some laughter. "OK, Dwight, tell you what, if you can get that car moved to Columbus we will write it up that it cannot move on its own wheels and you then can buy it for $300".

Talking with our friends in Transportation, they agreed to move the car to Columbus. It arrived at Columbus on February 8, 1996, on train R637, and was moved to a safe place for work to begin. After a couple of weeks of work, it was ready to move on down the old Hocking line to Nelsonville and the Hocking Valley Scenic Railway. It was delivered to the I&O at Parsons on February 28. On March 3 the Hocking Valley picked up the caboose from the I&O at Logan and moved it on to Nelsonville. We were now an official caboose owner!

C&O 903327 is shown at Walbridge on October 14, 1995, with SBD 16610 (acquired by the author in 1998) and 903323. Could this former Toledo Terminal caboose be saved? *Dwight Jones*

On February 23, 1996, work was continuing on the TT cab at Parsons Yard in Columbus. Primer paint was being rolled on and new "DT&I 100" reporting marks already had been applied for the future move to Nelsonville. This body style is the same as the first steel cabooses purchased by the DT&I. *Dwight Jones*

The "new" DT&I 100 is shown at Nelsonville on March 21, 1996, shortly after arrival and temporarily wearing a DT&I first-generation emblem. *Dwight Jones*

105

After full repainting into the DT&I scheme of the late 1960s, the car is shown at Nelsonville on July 28, 1996. After 10 years of caboose train service on the scenic rail line, the car was ready for a refurbishment in 2006. A new paint job and several other improvements are documented below. *Dwight Jones*

The author gave TT91 a 10 year refurbishment in 2006, repainting the car in a slightly older DT&I scheme which predated the newer scheme with the white side stripe. This older scheme also featured red cupola sides. As part of the refurbishment the car received a new smoke stack, end ladders were added which had been salvaged from a wood DT&I caboose that was being scrapped, doors were rebuilt on each end, and DT&I style window awnings were applied over the side windows. The car was renumbered one number higher than the DT&I's cars. This photo was taken at the conclusion of a caboose train trip on September 5, 2009, as happy riders detrain at the end of their four-hour journey, which included five photo runbys. *Dwight Jones*

Chapter 16

Safety Cabooses

Safety. That word has concerned management and employees for ages. And well if should, because safety is one of the most important assets an employee can possess. Recognizing this, management strives to encourage and promote safe employee practices at all times. Special bulletins, safety banners, messages in company newsletters, special contests, and timetable notices are just a few of the many ways the company has tried to drive home the safety message.

One of the more "colorful" mediums of safety communications developed by the Chessie System has been the "safety caboose". Painted in bright eye-catching colors and sporting a safety message on its side, a safety caboose is a rolling billboard that can take its safety message to any part of the system in a most unusual and highly-visible manner.

Chessie safety cabooses first were used on the B&O. In June 1973, B&O caboose C3025 emerged from the Du Bois, Pennsylvania, carshops with a bright red body and the safety message "YOUR FAMILY NEEDS YOU, STAY SAFE FOR THEM. How appropriate that the first color selected for a safety caboose would be red! The Du Bois shops continued to work on the safety caboose program and outshopped a total of 12 safety cabooses in 1973 and 1974.

To promote these new safety cabooses to the fullest, the company newsletter, *Chessie News*, announced a new employee safety contest. Employees were urged to be on the lookout for the 12 safety cabooses, record the date and place the cabooses were observed, the caboose number, color and safety message, and submit their list to the Director of Personal Injury Prevention in Baltimore. The first 5 employees to spot 10 of the 12 cars and send in their sightings correctly listing the cars would be awarded a special prize—a clock radio.

C&O and Western Maryland employees were at a decided disadvantage for this contest. B&O's bay-window cabooses as a general rule were not used in C&O and WM territories. The union agreements on the C&O, for example, required the use of a cupola caboose on C&O trains. So it came as no great surprise that the contest winner was a B&O employee—a brakeman at Parkersburg, West Virginia, who correctly identified 10 of the 12 cars by the August 1, 1974, deadline. Four runners up also were winners and received the clock radio prizes.

The concept of the safety caboose worked well on B&O because mainline cabooses were pooled. On C&O that was not the case. C&O cabooses were assigned to specific terminals and generally did not leave their respective territories. If safety cabooses were to appear on the C&O, they would have to maintain their division assignments. The C&O's Ohio Division Safety Committee realized this

Red Ohio Division safety caboose 3282 rests on the Mosel cab track at Columbus, Ohio, on May 16, 1976, six months after acquiring its unique attire at the Huntington car shops. *Dwight Jones*

and set the wheels in motion in 1975 to get four Ohio Division Safety Cabooses. Their request had to pass through various company channels for the necessary approvals, but all parties agreed it was a worthwhile project.

C&O Historical Society member, Chessie employee, and member of the Ohio Division Safety Committee Larry McNutt originally conceived the idea of safety cabooses on the Ohio Division. He explained to us that four assigned cabs were selected that would assure that all parts of the division would be exposed to a safety message:

3246 assigned Northern Subdivision manifests 97, 190
3282 assigned to the Carey Turn local
3285 assigned Columbus Subdiv. intradivisional pool
3287 assigned to the Nelsonville Turn local

The repainting of the four Ohio Division cars was assigned to the Huntington shops, which outshopped the four rainbow-hued cabooses in November and December of 1975.

The next safety cabooses to appear on Chessie rails were four Western Maryland cars that were painted at WM's Elkins, West Virginia, car shops in the fall of 1976. These cars originally were painted with small safety slogans that were judged unacceptable by management. The four cars were ordered back to the shops for repainting. Within a few short months three of the cars had been corrected. The fourth car, green 1803, managed to evade the Elkins painters for almost six years. It was finally repainted into the improved safety scheme in 1982. This car later was donated to the B&O Railroad Museum in Baltimore and was repainted at the museum into its updated version of the green safety scheme for museum display. In 2010 it wears the WM's colorful red/black/white scheme at the museum.

Two of the Western Maryland safety cabooses migrated off the WM to B&O and C&O assignments. Red 1811 spent some time on the B&O at Grafton, West Virginia, and eventually was sold to a private owner at Staunton, Virginia, where it remains. Of more interest to C&O fans, blue 1802 was sent to

Green 3285 is shown at Columbus on May 16, 1976. Lettering was applied in the same manner to both sides, as evidenced by "C"-3285 shown arriving at Hinton, West Virginia, with an eastbound train on April 24, 1982. Approvals for these specially painted cars was needed from several different departments. Nevertheless, we can't explain the confusion over the plural versus possessive form of "ACCIDENT".
All photos this page, Dwight Jones

Less than four months after receiving its "C" number prefix, blue "C"3246 is shown arriving at Russell from Columbus on November 22, 1979.

On June 23, 1980, orange C3287 had just arrived in Columbus from Walbridge, Ohio, with empty hoppers en route back to the West Virginia and Kentucky coalfields.

108   Steel Cabooses of the Chesapeake & Ohio

Columbus, Ohio, for local service in April 1982, working out of Parsons Yard. By 1987 it was in storage at Columbus, then was pulled from storage and repainted back to a WM speed-lettering scheme for a special convention display at Columbus. Thereafter it was donated to the Western Maryland Railway Historical Society at Union Bridge, Maryland.

One final batch of safety cabooses was completed in late 1976 for C&O. These cars were for service on the Michigan Division and included one car for Canadian District assignment. Like the Ohio Division cabooses, the Michigan Division, cars were strategically placed to give the most effective coverage to division employees:

3664 assigned to St. Thomas, Ontario
3143 assigned to Grand Rapids, Michigan
3163 assigned to Saginaw, Michigan

The final count for the safety caboose fleet was 23 cars. For the 1987 edition of this book, we reported that 10 of the cars had been repainted with their second coat of safety scheme paint. One B&O car even had been repainted three times. Some paint variations occurred on the repainted cars, such as C&O 3143, the only C&O car to be repainted. It was given yellow ends when repainted.

As the combined C&O/B&O system caboose pool was gradually implemented in the mid-1980s, the C&O's safety cabooses gave up their division assignments and, along with the B&O cabs, could show up at almost any location at any time. Unfortunately, caboose-less operations have taken a heavy toll on Chessie's safety caboose fleet. In January 1987 only 9 of the 23 original safety cabs were left in active service.

The Chessie's safety caboose concept was so popular that enthusiasts have repainted an additional three cars into similar schemes. Photos in this chapter cover those additional cars, which, in 2009, are the only ones left for photography.

The Bad Axe, Michigan, local was the assignment for gold 903163 when photographed on October 9, 1982, at Bad Axe. *Dwight Jones*

Since there were no wide-vision cabooses assigned to Canada, one of the C-15C cars was selected to be converted to a Canada safety caboose. C&O 903664, in orange paint, is shown on the St. Thomas, Ontario, caboose track on October 10, 1982. Notice that this was one of the first-generation steel cabooses that had its end window moved to the left of the door. It now has a steel plate sealing that opening. *Dwight Jones*

Cab 3143 is the only C&O caboose that was repainted into a second coat of safety paint. The green car, originally painted with aluminum ends, was repainted with much more attractive yellow ends. The car was photographed in local service at Grand Rapids, Michigan, on July 3, 1982. It was assigned to the "Kroger Job", and that stenciling appeared on the side of the car. *Dwight Jones*

Bad news for Bad Axe-assigned 903163. The car has been involved in a system accident and is shown on the shop track at Saginaw, Michigan, on May 25, 1986 with stenciling "Hold for Repairs 1-13-86". It subsequently was moved to Russell, Kentucky, for storage shortly after this photo was made. Later it was sold as scrap to Mansbach Metal at Ashland, Kentucky. *Dwight Jones*

Blue cabooses dominated the Mosel cab track when this photo was taken at the C&O's Parsons Yard, Columbus, Ohio, on May 16, 1976. Only two cabooses were in Chessie paint and they both were safety cabooses. *Dwight Jones*

110

Steel Cabooses of the Chesapeake & Ohio

An indication that division caboose pools had given way to a system caboose pool is Ohio Division green safety caboose C-3285 shown on April 24, 1982, on an eastbound coal train at Hinton, West Virginia. *Dwight Jones*

A coal train bound for Chicago rolls through the Ohio State University area at Columbus, Ohio, on March 14, 1982. Before the combining of C&O and B&O cabooses in a system pool, this train operated out of Columbus with both a B&O and C&O caboose. At Fostoria, Ohio, a B&O crew would take over and cut off the C&O caboose for the final leg of the journey to the Windy City. On this day, red safety caboose C3282 has the assignment with less-than-two-year-old B&O class C-27A 904012. *Dwight Jones*

Orange 3664 was the only class C-15C caboose repainted as a safety caboose, for service in Canada. Its celebrity status was short-lived as the car was burned to a crisp. It is shown in this photo in storage at Oak Yard in Detroit on July 4, 1985. Ironically, of 23 safety cabooses, three of the cars were destroyed by fire. As one yardmaster friend put it, "It's not a pretty sight". *Dwight Jones*

End of the line for orange safety caboose 903287 shown on the ground at Mansbach Metal, Ashland, Kentucky. This caboose was scheduled to be part of a new railroad park at Ashland. Its trucks already had been moved to the special panel display track when this March 16, 1996, photo was taken. A change in city management canceled the project and the caboose subsequently was scrapped. Fortunately, the author was given permission to remove all of the windows, and other miscellaneous parts, to support the refurbishment of DT&I wide-vision caboose 142, now on display at Jackson, Ohio. *Dwight Jones*

The most recent caboose to join the fraternity of the "safety cabooses" is C&O 3316. The car was acquired by a private owner from a museum. The new owner patterned his version after the original 3163, repainting it yellow-gold. It is displayed near Pelham, Georgia, where it was photographed on May 3, 2009. *Dwight Jones*

112 Steel Cabooses of the Chesapeake & Ohio

For the 1993 C&O Historical Society Conference, held at Columbus, conference manager Dick Argo wondered if a caboose could be specially painted to be part of a planned Parsons Yard equipment display. The author suggested a tribute to the Chessie safety caboose, since 1993 would mark the 20th anniversary of the introduction of the idea on Chessie. The conference planning committee approved the idea and locally-assigned caboose 903180 was selected for the honor. Jacksonville CSX officials approved the project with the understanding that after the conference was over, the caboose would be revised slightly to become a "CSX" safety caboose.

Above, the specially-painted safety caboose was used as the backdrop for the annual group photo of conference attendees. Special lettering on this side only paid tribute to the 1993 conference. At left, what the car looked like during the Parsons Yard tour without the posed crowd. Both photos were taken on July 23, 1993.

Below, this is how the Chessie System version looked with the safety slogan in the white band along the roof. This side was painted green while the opposite side of the car was painted light purple. A slogan applied just below the cupola paid tribute to the 20th anniversary of the safety cabooses. After the conference the C&O lettering on the cupola side was replaced with CSXT markings, the safety emblem was replaced by the then-current CSX safety lantern emblem and the Chess-C emblem and Chessie System lettering were replaced with a large CSX monogram. Still later the railroad asked the author to replace the safety lantern emblem with the circular C&O Business Unit logo. This caboose still remains in local service at Columbus as this is being written in 2009, 16 years after it was painted for the conference. It is heavily weathered and in need of repainting. Who knows, maybe at the next Columbus conference it will get that repainting. In December 2009 the car was reassigned to local service as a shoving platform at Fostoria, Ohio. C&OHS members who helped paint the car in 1993 included Luther George, Dwight Jones, Ted Wetterstroem, Mike Meister. and Ron Weaver. *all this page,* Dwight Jones

Chessie System Safety Cabooses

RR	Original Number	Original Color	First-Painted Date	Shop	Safety Slogan
B&O	C3000	Green	6-21-73	DU	BE ALERT, DON'T GET HURT
B&O	C3003	White	11-1-73	DU	LONG CHANCES SHORTEN LIVES
B&O	C3010	Gold	1-11-74	DU	SAFETY IS A FULL-TIME JOB
B&O	C3017	Maroon	4-18-74	DU	SAFETY & SERVICE-WE WORK FOR BOTH
B&O	C3025	Red	6-15-73	DU	YOUR FAMILY NEEDS YOU, STAY SAFE FOR THEM
B&O	C3028	Blue	12-11-73	DU	SAFE TODAY-HERE TOMORROW
B&O	C3035	Lt. Blue	11-21-73	DU	KEEP SAFETY IN MIND ALL OF THE TIME
B&O	C3043	Orange	1-31-74	DU	SAFETY IS OF FIRST IMPORTANCE
B&O	C3714	Brown	5- -74	DU	CHESSIE HAS NINE LIVES, YOU HAVE ONE-BE SAFE
B&O	C3718	Purple	5-10-74	DU	SAFETY IS NO ACCIDENT
B&O	C3771	Tan	3-13-74	DU	SAFETY IS NOT A PART-TIME JOB
B&O	C3774	Lt. Green	3- -74	DU	SAFETY IS NO MYSTERY JUST COMMON SENSE
C&O	3246	Blue	12-4-75	HTG	WEEKLY SAFETY SLOGAN WHAT'S THIS WEEK'S
C&O	3282	Red	11-21-75	HTG	MAKE THIS YEAR A SAFER YEAR
C&O	3285	Green	12-28-75	HTG	NEAR-MISS PROGRAM X OUT ACCIDENT'S
C&O	3287	Orange	12-15-75	HTG	SAFETY IS FREE USE IT
WM	1802	Blue	9- -76	ELK	LEAD, FOLLOW OR CLEAR THE WAY FOR SAFETY
WM	1803	Green	10-15-76	ELK	NEAR-MISS PROGRAM, ARE YOU DOING YOUR PART?
WM	1806	Orange	10-15-76	ELK	WORK BY YOUR SAFETY RULES
WM	1811	Red	9- -76	ELK	SAFETY! IS IT FIRST IN YOUR MIND?
C&O	3143	Green	11-9-76	GR	SAFETYS DIVIDENDS ARE PRICELESS
C&O	3163	Gold	12-10-76	GR	LAST IN THE TRAIN BUT FIRST IN SAFETY
C&O	3664	Orange	10-28-76	GR	SAFETY IS GOOD FOR LIFE
C&O	3180	Note 1	7-93	Columbus	see Note 1
B&O	C3842	Note 2	4-95	Columbus	see Note 2
C&O	3316	Lt. Gold	4-09	Note 3	LAST IN THE TRAIN BUT FIRST IN SAFETY

Note 1: Caboose 903180 was specially painted for the 1993 C&O Historical Society Conference
Note 2: B&O C3842 was another of the author's repaint projects for the B&O Railroad Museum
Note 3: C&O 3316 was modeled after original 3163 by a private owner for his Georgia display
Note 4: C&O 3143 was repainted into a second safety slogan scheme at Grand Rapids 6-81

C&O Safety Caboose Paint Schemes

	3282	3285	3246	3287	3143 (1st)	3143 (2nd)	3163	3664
Body Color >	RED	GREEN	BLUE	ORANGE	GREEN	GREEN	GOLD	ORANGE
DuPont Body Color #	#19	#94	#68	#14	#94	unknown	#10	#14
Grabirons >	YELLOW	YELLOW	YELLOW	YELLOW	YELLOW	WHITE	YELLOW	YELLOW
Trucks >	BLACK	BLACK	BLACK	BLACK	ALUMIN.	BLACK	ALUMIN.	ALUMIN.
Underframe >	ALUMIN.	ALUMIN.	ALUMIN.	ALUMIN.	ALUMIN.	BLACK	ALUMIN.	ALUMIN.
Lettering >	Note 1	Note 1	Note 1	Note 5	BLACK	Note 2	BLUE	BLACK
Smokestack >	ALUMIN.	ALUMIN.	ALUMIN.	ALUMIN.	ALUMIN.	ALUMIN.	ALUMIN.	ALUMIN.
End Platform >	ALUMIN.	ALUMIN.	ALUMIN.	ALUMIN.	ALUMIN.	ALUMIN.	ALUMIN.	ALUMIN.
Roof >	ALUMIN.	ALUMIN.	ALUMIN.	ALUMIN.	ALUMIN.	ALUMIN.	ALUMIN.	ALUMIN.
Body/Cupola Ends >	ALUMIN.	ALUMIN.	ALUMIN.	ALUMIN.	ALUMIN.	YELLOW	ALUMIN.	ALUMIN.
Roof Sideplate >	ALUMIN.	ALUMIN.	ALUMIN.	ALUMIN.	ALUMIN.	WHITE	ALUMIN.	ALUMIN.
Steps >	ALUMIN.	ALUMIN.	ALUMIN.	ALUMIN.	ALUMIN.	BLACK	ALUMIN.	ALUMIN.
See Note Below >					Note 7	Note 3	Note 7	Note 7
Front Edge of Step Treads	YELLOW	ALUMIN.	YELLOW	YELLOW	YELLOW	WHITE	YELLOW	YELLOW

Note 1: White on body, black on white slogan background and cupola ends
Note 2: Yellow on green, blue on white, green on yellow
Note 3: Bottom side stripe-white; ends of roof-white; end doors-green
Note 4: Safety emblem: green cross, white background, black tracks
Note 5: Blue side lettering; black lettering on cupola ends and on white safety slogan background
Note 6: All safety slogan backgrounds-white
Note 7: Body window frames-aluminum

Steel Cabooses of the Chesapeake & Ohio

Chapter 17

CCH Cabooses

CCH (Careful Car Handling) cabooses were a 1982 creation of Chessie's Freight Damage Prevention Department in a systemwide effort to awaken employees to the escalating problem of freight damage caused by rough train handling practices.

Caboose cars used as rolling, eye-catching billboards were the main feature of the program. Colorful posters were distributed systemwide to all terminal locations and other points. The posters enticed employees with the promise of a "reward" of a free CCH ball cap to those who spotted a roaming CCH caboose and sent their sighting to the Freight Damage Prevention Department in Baltimore.

The cabooses chosen for the CCH program were painted in specially selected colors for easy spotting and high visibility around the system.

CCH Caboose Colors
OSHA "Safety Orange"—carbody side and ends
Enchantment Blue—roof, smokestack, steps, and underframe
White—grabirons, end railings, chains and lettering
Signal Yellow—roof side plate, cupola side plate, and bottom side stripe
Black and white decals—CCH insignia and slogan
Black—trucks

The paint and lettering scheme was designed by the Chessie Graphics Department, although the CCH insignia is not a Chessie design. It is somewhat of a universal symbol for damage prevention and is believed to have originated on the Canadian National.

The first car of the project, 903118, was painted in June 1982 at the Grand Rapids, Michigan, shops. That initial cab was followed by two more C&O cars, which also were painted at Grand Rapids. These three cars were sent out to roam the far corners of the C&O, and were carefully controlled by the Transportation Department in Baltimore to assure

C&O C3118 (above left) was wearing a standard coat of Chessie yellow on May 4, 1980, with an eastbound manifest on B&O tracks at Cincinnati. Two years later the car posed in fresh paint at the Grand Rapids, Michigan, shops on July 3, 1982, as the first of six **C&O/B&O orange CCH cabooses.** *both, Dwight Jones*

that all parts of the C&O would get exposure to them.

On the B&O side, things did not move along as smoothly. Through poor coordination, inadequate planning, or just bad timing, it was five months after the first C&O car was painted that the first B&O car was given the CCH treatment.

Although system caboose work was under way at the Raceland car shops (where B&O cabs normally underwent heavy repairs and painting during this era), the B&O cabs selected for this CCH program were sent to the Cumberland, Maryland, shops where their interiors were painted. The cabs then were shipped to the B&O's Brunswick, Maryland, shops for exterior painting—a strange move since the Cumberland shops were doing freight car painting at the time. Possibly some union agreement dictated this odd situation.

En route from Cumberland to Brunswick, one cab was inadvertently put back into active caboose service and had to be tracked down again and routed to Brunswick. Coincidentally, economic conditions had eroded on the railroad front to the point that massive furloughs at Chessie shops, including Brunswick, resulted in that last car being stranded at the shops for almost half a year. In fact, that last B&O caboose did not get the CCH colors until well after the CCH program had officially ended in December 1982!

The B&O cars were further jinxed when car 903747 sustained interior fire damage around April 1983 (ironic when one considers that this CCH cab was to promote careful car handling!). The fire-damaged car subsequently was placed in storage at Cumberland, where it remained until early 1986, when it and 903758 were retired.

This end view of caboose 903103, at Russell, Kentucky, on September 18, 1982, shows application of the orange, white grabirons and the yellow stripe along the bottom of the roof end. The car number shows above the end window. *Dwight Jones*

C&O 903237, shown arriving at Columbus, Ohio, on November 13, 1983, with an eastbound empties train, was still in the blue paint scheme and was stored at Grand Rapids when it was selected to be C&O's third and final CCH caboose. *Dwight Jones*

116   Steel Cabooses of the Chesapeake & Ohio

Chessie's CCH Cabooses

Cab #	Road	Painted Date	Painted Shop
903118	C&O	6-82	Grand Rapids, MI
903103	C&O	8-82	Grand Rapids, MI
903237	C&O	9-82	Grand Rapids, MI
903747	B&O	11-82	Brunswick, MD
903758	B&O	11-82	Brunswick, MD
903820	B&O	4-83	Brunswick, MD

Full-color CCH posters were distributed system-wide to alert employees to watch for the colorful cabooses. The reward of a CCH ball cap was depicted on the poster. The original of the poster at right was presented to the author by T.J. Schoenleben when the author was researching the cabooses in Chessie corporate offices at Baltimore. Mr. Schoenleben was the point person for this project as can be seen by his contact information shown on the poster bottom. *Dwight Jones*

As viewed from the yardmaster's office, "C&O High Tower", CCH caboose 903103 shares space on the ash pit track with yard cabs C90340 and 900979 at Columbus on March 13, 1983. *Dwight Jones*

117

This lineup of cabooses on the west end of the Light Side caboose track at Russell on September 18, 1982, looks like the cars were posed deliberately by the Public Relations Department. Three different wide-vision paint schemes are shown. At left is the C3238, still retaining its original blue scheme. Freshly painted CCH caboose 903103 is shown in the middle, with 903324 in relatively fresh Chessie yellow on the right. This view is a good way to illustrate the bright fresh image that the Chessie System scheme brought to the railroad, as opposed to the older solid blue scheme. *Dwight Jones*

Three B&O cabooses also received the CCH colors including 903758, which was photographed in the process of being repainted at the Brunswick, Maryland, shops on December 5, 1982. *Dwight Jones*

An in-service 903758 teamed up with C&O bay-window caboose 904109 at showcase Queensgate Yard, Cincinnati, on January 8, 1983. *Dwight Jones*

118

Steel Cabooses of the Chesapeake & Ohio

Chapter 18

Solar Cabooses

In late 1980 a caboose emerged from the C&O shops at Grand Rapids, Michigan, with an unusual device mounted on the cupola roof. It was a solar panel, and with that initial application, space-age technology had finally come to the ranks of the Chessie caboose fleet.

The Grand Rapids shops followed up that initial solar cab with two more cupola caboose applications and one bay-window caboose installation. One additional B&O bay-window pool caboose was equipped with solar panels at the Raceland, Kentucky, car shops.

Chessie's solar panel applications were nothing unique in the railroad industry. Over a half dozen roads have applied solar devices to lineside signals, grade crossing protectors, radio repeaters, and cabooses. Even refrigerator cars have been examined for feasible applications.

Cabooses used in local service, yard duty, and on mine runs were particularly well-suited candidates for the solar additions. They had minimal electrical requirements—most had little more than an FRA light, backup light, and radio to power. Indeed, solar panels were installed on at least 80 locally-assigned Southern Railway cabooses.

Solar panels, which date back to the late 1950s, came into their own in the early 1970s when the energy crunch brought about increased research and development to locate alternate energy supplies. By the 1980s, solar panels had evolved into neatly packaged units of photovoltaic cells that convert sunlight directly into electricity.

Lack of moving parts is a particular advantage for use in railroad operations. The mechanical components so prone to failure and maintenance on conventional end-of-axle-mounted generators or belt-driven units are completely eliminated on solar applications. In a solar system the batteries, solar panels, voltage regulator, and some wiring are the only basic appurtenances that are required.

The five original Chessie solar cabooses:

Cab #	Road	Equipped Date	Shop	Assignment
1814	WM	10-31-80	GR	B&OCT Yard Service
90214	C&O	12-10-80	GR	Martin, KY, mine run
900287	C&O	11-13-81	GR	Raleigh, WV, mine run
904155	C&O	2-2-82	GR	Plymouth, MI, local
903716	B&O	3-12-82	RA	System caboose pool

As can be seen from the table, the solar cabs were carefully distributed around the system to test their performance under varied conditions. Two cars went into coalfield service on mine runs, one car into yard service, one car to Michigan Division assignment, and the final car to roam the system in pool service.

It appeared that Chessie's solar caboose experiment was a

Solar panels installed on Chessie's bay-window cabooses were of much larger capacity than those applied to the cupola cars. C&O 904155 was photographed at Plymouth, Michigan, on May 27, 1983. *Dwight Jones*

success. The only known problem was when caboose 90214 was operated under a close-clearance tipple and had some of its panels damaged. The panels were replaced at the Russell shops and the car returned to service. With the elimination of cabooses there was no need to expand application on a grand scale.

Solar panel application to cabooses 90214 and 900287 was virtually identical. The 900287 was photographed at Raleigh on April 24, 1982. The 90214 was photographed on April 9, 1982, at Martin, Kentucky. *Dwight Jones*

C&O 900287 is shown at its assigned location at Raleigh, West Virginia, on April 24, 1982, with a couple of sister cabooses. *Dwight Jones*

Solar panels remained on 900214 and 900287 until the cabs were removed from service. The panels were removed from 904155 and 904131 when converted to shoving platforms in 1991 and 2002 respectively.

C&O railroading at its best: mountains, blue geeps, black hoppers, and Kentucky coal—somehow solar panel-equipped 90214 seems oddly out of place at Martin, Kentucky, on April 9, 1982. *Dwight Jones*

By 1986 some assigned cabooses had been released to the system caboose pool. C&O 904155 is a long way from its original Michigan assignment—it is pictured at Grafton, West Virginia, on March 22, 1986, on an eastbound coal train. A pair of helpers sit in the background on the Hill Track. *Dwight Jones*

C&O caboose 903563, assigned at Columbus to the "B&O Puller" had fallen into a state of disrepair by early 1999 and needed to be replaced. Division officers sent C&O 904131 as a replacement. Imagine our surprise, when the car arrived in February 1999, to see that it had been equipped for solar operation.

In researching the history of this application, we found that it had been given the solar equipment at the South Charleston, West Virginia, car shops around 1994. The car was being used between Seth and Prenter, West Virginia, and the car's generator was not keeping the electrical system properly supplied. The solar panels were an extra set that had been in the stores department at Shelby, Kentucky, to support the original two mine run cabs 90214 and 900287. This car also was equipped with an external electrical cord which was located on one side and had a male plug on the end. (It was located by the "h" in Chessie). This cord was used to plug into a lineside battery charger at Seth. This cord was removed at Columbus about a week after this April 1999 photo was taken.

In order to get an overhead shot of this application local officials cooperated by placing a locomotive so we could climb onto the low nose for this photo. Note the backup light installed on the roof end. See page 96 for more information on this car leaving Columbus. *Dwight Jones*

121

Chapter 19

Painting and Lettering

Probably no part of equipment history is of greater importance to modelers than painting and lettering practices. Historians are likewise fascinated with this history. The subject is both interesting and confusing. At times it appears that there was no rhyme or reason to railroad paint and lettering practices. Variations to "standard" schemes seem numerous. Even variations of the variations seemed to occur. To gain a better understanding of these instances, it is necessary to examine how most railroads communicate paint and lettering instructions to their shops and painters.

On the C&O, Mechanical Department headquarters (at Cleveland during A.M.C. days, then Richmond, then Huntington until 1986) would prepare a lettering diagram that was issued to car shops that might be painting a particular type of car. In addition to a schematic of the car showing lettering placement, type, and car colors, there usually was a list of each drawing number for all numerals, monograms, and letters. These latter drawings were made full size for easy one-to-one conversion to stencils by each car shop. Some drawings would even specify the paint number and primer to be used. If paint colors and manufacturer codes were not listed on the lettering drawing, they were contained in separate painting specifications. With all of these instructions how could a paint or lettering variation occur?

There are many reasons. Sometimes, for instance, a caboose would be painted at a shop that did not normally do caboose work, and the necessary diagrams and stencils might not be available at that shop. Instructions, no matter how clear, are only as good as the person interpreting them. We wonder if some variations were done deliberately at the whim of the painter or car foreman. One could probably document as many reasons for paint and lettering variations as there are cabooses on the roster. The variations were not confined to the pre-Chessie era. Many of the most interesting have occurred during the Chessie years.[15]

Throughout this book we have tried to identify paint and lettering variations carefully by coding representative photographs with (STD) for standard schemes and (NON-STD) for schemes considered to be nonstandard. But nonstandard compared to what? That brings up another difficult question. Does one consider a standard scheme one that has been approved and issued by the Mechanical Department, or one that is more or less universally applied by system car shops? And no, they were not always the same. Here are some examples. B&O's Du Bois, Pennsylvania, shops painted many B&O cabooses into the Chessie scheme. We never observed one car from that shop that had vermilion window frames, even though they were clearly specified to be vermilion on painting and lettering drawings. Not until Du Bois was closed and B&O caboose work was transferred to Raceland did B&O cabooses begin emerging with vermilion window frames. But, we have never seen a cab emerge from Raceland (either C&O or B&O) with anything but an aluminum smokestack—although they were clearly specified to be painted Enchantment Blue. The Chessie scheme called for roofs to be painted aluminum, but all of the 90200/90300 series cars that we observed from the Grand Rapids shops had light gray roofs. And so it goes.[16]

To be consistent, in this book we have considered "Standard" to mean "approved and issued by the Mechanical Department".

Modelers need not shy away from the oddities. Just as they give the prototype fan an interesting break from the "fleet appearance", they similarly can give the modeler a unique (and prototypically accurate) conversation piece.

Tabulated in this chapter are "standard" paint and lettering data for C&O steel cabooses. Compiled from official C&O paint and lettering diagrams, C&O painting specifications, photos, and personal observations, these are the schemes applied to the vast majority of C&O steel cabooses over the past five decades.[17]

An additional note: This may seem elementary to some, but, when changes to paint and lettering schemes were made, all cars were not called into the shops the following day to be repainted. It took years for all cars to be affected. In fact, some changes were made often enough that there might be cars in service with several different schemes at any given time. That explains why, for instance, some cabooses survived into the 1960s still retaining their Pere Marquette lettering in the red scheme or wearing their C&O red scheme. In 1986 there were 31 wide-vision cabooses in service on C&O still wearing their original blue scheme. They had evaded company painters for nearly 14 years. And as we work on this update in early 2009, one of those cars still is in service on CSX in its original blue scheme—37 years after the scheme was superseded by Chessie yellow.

Those Caboose Blues

It was quite a change when C&O caboose 3100 emerged from

continued on page 124

This C&O photo of 90001 shows the car on display at Richmond, Virginia, at C&O's 17th Street yard on April 4, 1956, and wearing what was described as an "experimental yellow" scheme, for the 1956 C&O Stockholderama. This is believed to be the first caboose painted in the yellow scheme. This side illustrates the scheme that actually was adopted by C&O management. The opposite side was painted in a different yellow scheme (see page 31 for that scheme). The June 1956 *Tracks Magazine*, carrying the story of the 1956 Stockholderama, reported the following:

> And the traditional little red caboose on the C&O will blossom out in a new color scheme of bright yellow if the railroad's officers and shareholders like a sample which was unveiled at the Annual Meeting and Stockholderama. Greater visibility—and therefore safety—is the objective of a yellow caboose, with red lettering

We are not sure where they came up with that reference to "red lettering". Most likely the C&O writer was referring to the red side stripe along the bottom and the red safety appliances.

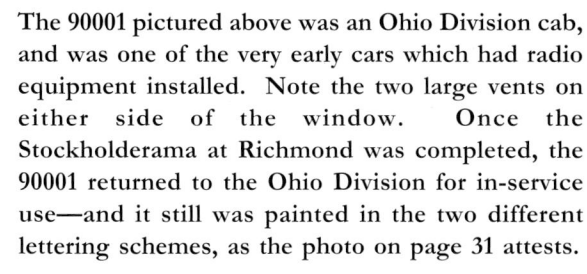

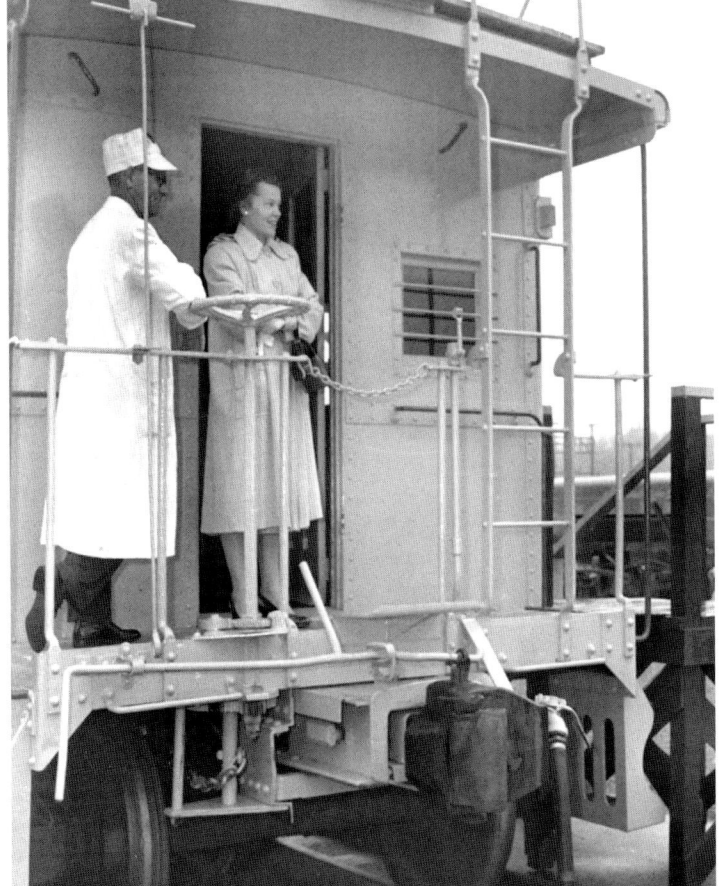

The 90001 pictured above was an Ohio Division cab, and was one of the very early cars which had radio equipment installed. Note the two large vents on either side of the window. Once the Stockholderama at Richmond was completed, the 90001 returned to the Ohio Division for in-service use—and it still was painted in the two different lettering schemes, as the photo on page 31 attests.

At left is another view of the 90001 on display at Richmond. A C&O technician, dressed in a white lab coat, is on hand for safety purposes and to respond to any questions that visitors might have. In this early scheme the end railings were painted yellow and the end and side grabirons were red. The grabirons were apparently repainted before the car returned to service, but the two different lettering schemes remained. *C&OHS Collection*

continued from page 122

the International Car paint shop in July 1968, debuting the new all-blue caboose paint scheme. Several opinions have surfaced over the years to explain the rationale for adopting blue as the primary caboose color. Probably the most accurate account is that the blue scheme was adopted to be consistent with arch-rival Norfolk and Western.[18]

C&O and N&W put their competitiveness aside and began merger rumblings in 1965 as a defense to the combining of New York Central and the Pennsylvania Railroad. N&W+C&O won an ICC examiner's approval in the spring of 1969. Internally, company officials were confident that a merger of the two coal haulers would be approved. They were so confident, in fact, that tangible changes began appearing. Among the most noteworthy on the C&O side was the renumbering, in 1970, of SD18 and U25B locomotives to N&W series numbers.

The adoption of a primarily-blue paint scheme for C&O/B&O cabooses is said to have occurred because N&W cabooses were blue.[19] This story was confirmed to us by a CSX mechanical department official who was working with paint and lettering schemes in the C&O mechanical department in the late 1960s.

A nervous ICC reopened the N&W+C&O case in the summer of 1970 to study possible negative effects on Penn Central. In the spring of 1971 the N&W and C&O boards voted to cancel the affiliation. N&W wasted no time revising their paint and lettering schemes. They adopted the large NW lettering and the color red for caboose cars circa 1971. C&O/B&O came out with the Chessie System image a year later in late 1972.

Missing Red Frame Stripes

Throughout this book there are many photos of cabooses in the yellow paint scheme that are apparently lacking the prominent red frame stripe. We submit that there are two reasons for that anomaly:

Some cabooses painted in the late 1960s and early 1970s were painted with a nonstandard fluorescent-type red paint. It looked good when first applied, and the reasoning for its use at the time was sound—improved visibility with some reflectance properties. However, the paint seemed to fade away very quickly. The new paint just could not withstand the elements.

The second reason is that the railroad did not apply the red side stripe. We are not sure what the reason was for this but

N&W caboose 518452, one of 15 class C-3 cars purchased from International Railway Car Company in 1958, is shown modeling the N&W's blue caboose scheme, which is said to have been the model for the C&O/B&O blue caboose scheme. Note the yellow diagonal end stripes—also adopted, to a lesser extent, on C&O/B&O cabooses. *Paul Dunn Collection*

The last three cabooses to be painted into the Chessie System scheme were these three cabs shown inside the Raceland, Kentucky, paint shop on September 1, 1985. On this date cabooses 903141 and 903149 needed only minor touchup work to be complete—they were released shortly after this photo was taken. The last cab to receive Chessie livery, 903311, was released from the shops in late September 1985. *Dwight Jones*

we have examined enough photos showing this condition that the conclusion is that this was quite common during that era.

Color photos in this book, such as the C&O's own photo of ex Western Maryland 90350, clearly show.

Those hallowed halls at Grand Rapids. As the chart in this chapter shows, more C&O cabooses have received major repairs and painting at Grand Rapids during the Chessie era than at any other Chessie car facility. Trucks are removed for inspection of critical parts. *Dwight Jones*

Aluminum Grabirons and Railings (1958)

The Paint Color Chart in this chapter indicates that grabirons were painted aluminum beginning in January 1959. A letter now has been discovered, which was issued by the C&O Mechanical Department at Richmond, June 23, 1958, which sheds some additional light on this caboose painting change. Parts of the letter are extracted below:

"Further in connection with your file concerning painting of safety appliances and sill steps of newly painted yellow caboose cars with aluminum paint.

"The following caboose cars have had the grab irons and sill steps painted aluminum and are operating on the Northern, Central, and Eastern Regions.

A804	90042	90115	90180	90244	90349
A822	90051	90117	90182	90247	90776
A910	90052	90129	90196	90248	90778
A956	90085	90137	90219	90266	90814
A977	90086	90151	90222	90279	90875
A978	90089	90152	90229	90305	90909
90028	90091	90166	90239	90345	90942

"We are assuming that you will have above cabooses inspected on the various regions so that we may obtain the reactions of the local people. We will appreciate your comments as to the continuance of painting cabooses in this manner."

A Columbus, Ohio, trainmaster responded to the above letter with his letter which was dated July 29, 1958, parts of which are reproduced below:

"At 5:20 P.M., July 23, Asst. Trainmaster Ernie VonSchriltz and I observed caboose 90180 at Parsons terminal and it is our combined opinion that the painting of the grabirons and sill steps is a vast improvement over the old method."

This letter provides a couple of interesting points of interest to C&O fans. First, the railroad was painting cabooses from red into the new yellow scheme at the rate of about one car per week.

And secondly, this shows that car color changes sometimes do not match up exactly with drawing revision dates as it is clear that cabooses were being painted with aluminum grabirons and railings long before the drawing revision date.

C&O / PM Paint Color Chart[20]

Dates below are beginning dates for color changes to car categories listed in the left column

Applicable Cars > / Body Part	8-37	9-41	4-47	5-57	Note 10	1-59	7-68	9-72	4-80
	ALL STEEL CABOOSES						Note 4	Note 8	C-27A
Body	RED			YELLOW			BLUE	YELLOW	YELLOW
Grabirons	BLACK	Note 3		GREEN		ALMNM.	YELLOW	VRMLN.	WHITE
Trucks	BLACK			BLACK			BLACK	BLUE	BLUE
Underframe	BLACK			BLACK			BLACK	BLUE	BLUE
Lettering	WHITE			BLUE			Note 5	Note 7	Note 7
Smokestack	BLACK			GRAY			BLUE	BLUE	BLUE
End Platform	BLACK	Note 9	BLACK	GRAY			BLUE	YELLOW	BLUE
Roof	BLACK			GRAY			Note 6	ALMNM.	ALMNM.
Side stripe(s)				RED			YELLOW	VRMLN.	VRMLN.
See Note >							Note 2	Note 1	Note 12
Steps	BLACK			GREEN		Note 11	BLUE	BLUE	BLUE
Step Treads	BLACK			GRAY			BLUE	BLUE	YELLOW
Front Edge of Step Treads					YELLOW	ALMNM.	YELLOW	VRMLN.	WHITE

The C&O painting specification of 1947 stated the following: "Platform floor and inside of platform steps shall be given three coats of metallic brown paint. Two coats of black paint shall be applied to platform and sills." (Refer to the color photos in the back of this book.)

Note 1: End doors painted blue; window frames-aluminum.
Note 2: Roof ends painted yellow with red diagonal stripes.
Note 3: Body side grabirons, body end grabirons and corner posts extending from roof to platform-yellow; balance of grabirons, ladder, columns, railings-black.
Note 4: C-15C, C-25 cars only.
Note 5: White on black background, yellow on blue background.
Note 6: Aluminum on C-25 cars, blue on C-15C cars.
Note 7: Blue lettering on yellow background, yellow lettering on blue background.
Note 8: All cabooses except class C-27A.
Note 9: Color unknown but not black. Perhaps red or brown.
Note 10: Aluminum superceded by yellow 1-59 but exact start date for yellow has not been determined.
Note 11: Black steps were in use after this date but exact start date has not been determined.
Note 12: End doors-blue; safety emblem: white background, black tracks, green cross.

Chart Abbreviations:

YELLOW = Signal Yellow   BLUE = Enchantment Blue
ALMNM. = Aluminum   VRMLN. = Vermilion

Pre 11/54 monogram   Post 11/54 monogram   Post 9/72 monogram

C&O / PM Lettering Chart

Scheme Number	Issue Date	Description of Lettering	Refer to Photo Caboose No.	Page
		PERE MARQUETTE		
1	9/37	"PERE MARQUETTE" and car number centered on car sides in 9" high Roman figures. "PM" and car number centered on each end above door in 4" high Roman figures.	A901	15
		CHESAPEAKE & OHIO		
2	7/37	9" high "CHESAPEAKE & OHIO" and 7" high car number centered on car sides in Roman figures. Car number centered over each end door in 4" high Roman figures.	A911 90000	16 29
3	12/48	Same as scheme #2 except C&O first generation monogram added for cars 90200-90349.	90609	11
4	6/49	Same as scheme #3 except size of "CHESAPEAKE & OHIO" changed to 7" size letters and C&O monogram made applicable to all steel cabooses.	90299	42
5	11/54	Same as scheme #4 except C&O monogram changed to second generation style. See cover photo for first generation emblem.	A918	146
6	5/57	Removed "CHESAPEAKE & OHIO" from car sides and 4" high car numbers above end doors. Changed size of caboose numbers on car sides to 9" and changed style of letters and numerals to Futura Demibold. Added last three digits of road number (full road number for former PM cars) in 9" high figures to both ends of cupola. (new yellow body scheme)	90675	56
7	10/57	Changed position of numbers and figures on cupola ends to locate top of figures flush with top of cupola windows.	90236	44
8	7/68	C&O monogram on each side of car. Car number in 9" high Futura Demibold figures centered on cupola sides (C-25 cars) or just below cupola window (C-15C cars) and on cupola ends with top of number flush with top of cupola windows. Note: This scheme applied only to class C-25 and C-15C cars. (new blue scheme)	3100 3675	68 82
9	9/72	Large "Chessie System" applied to side of each car per following: 40" Chess-C emblem on C-25 cabs, 32" Chess-C on all other steel cupola cabooses. Railroad initials and car number applied using 9" figures in stacked fashion to ends of cupola (only C-15C and C-25 cabooses; older steel cabs received railroad initials and only the last three road number digits on cupola ends). Railroad initials and full road number applied using 9" figures to both sides of car on a single line, not stacked.	3322	77
10	6/79	Instructions issued to add letter "C" as a prefix to caboose numbers. "C&O" initials on car sides had to be moved to the left and "C" prefix added to road number. No change made to cupola numbers on previously-Chessied cabooses. Those cars remaining in blue were to have "C&O" initials applied in stacked fashion over the cupola road number digits.	C-3180	79
11	4/80	Safety emblem on each side to right of bay. Railroad initials applied above baywindow in 12" figures. Road number applied with 9" figures below baywindow, and on end of roof with 5" figures. To left of baywindow on smokestack side of car, 53" Chess-C emblem and 12 "Chessie System" are applied. On opposite side of car, to left of baywindow, "Chessie System" lettering is applied below three side windows using 20" Chess-C emblem.	904094	91
12	1/82	Instructions revised to renumber cabooses to 900000 series as follows: "C&O" initials were to be applied in stacked fashion over six digit road number on sides of cupola (C-25 cars), and on sides of caboose just under cupola window on other steel cupola cabooses.	903152 903595	72 88

Paint Shops for the Chessie Scheme

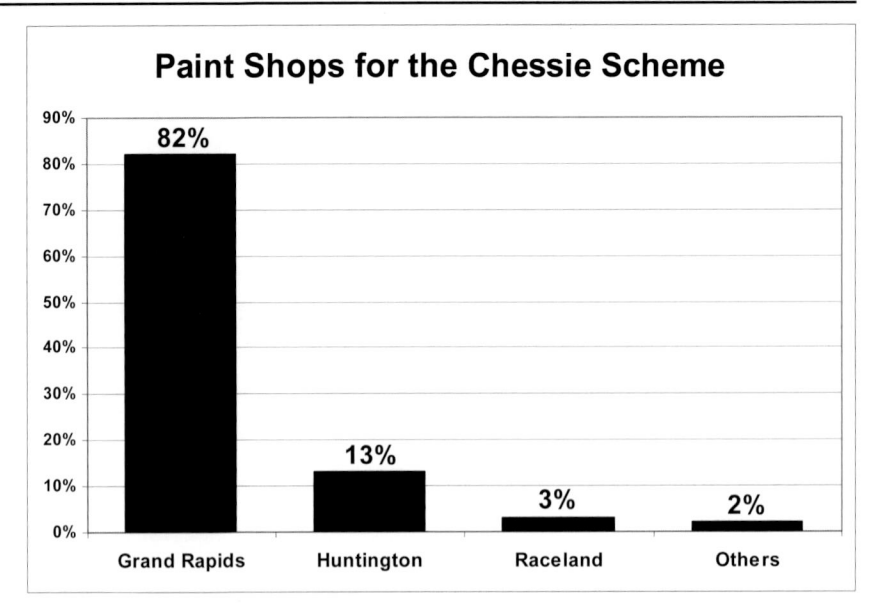

Shop	Percentage
Grand Rapids	82%
Huntington	13%
Raceland	3%
Others	2%

If ever there was a doubt about the number one C&O caboose shop during the Chessie era, the graph above should clearly provide an answer. Graphed were shop codes from 488 C&O cabooses that had been repainted into the Chessie scheme and that carried a stenciled shop code. The chart shows what percentage of the 488 cabooses was repainted at each shop. The "Others" category includes smaller shops such as Walbridge, Stevens and Chicago.

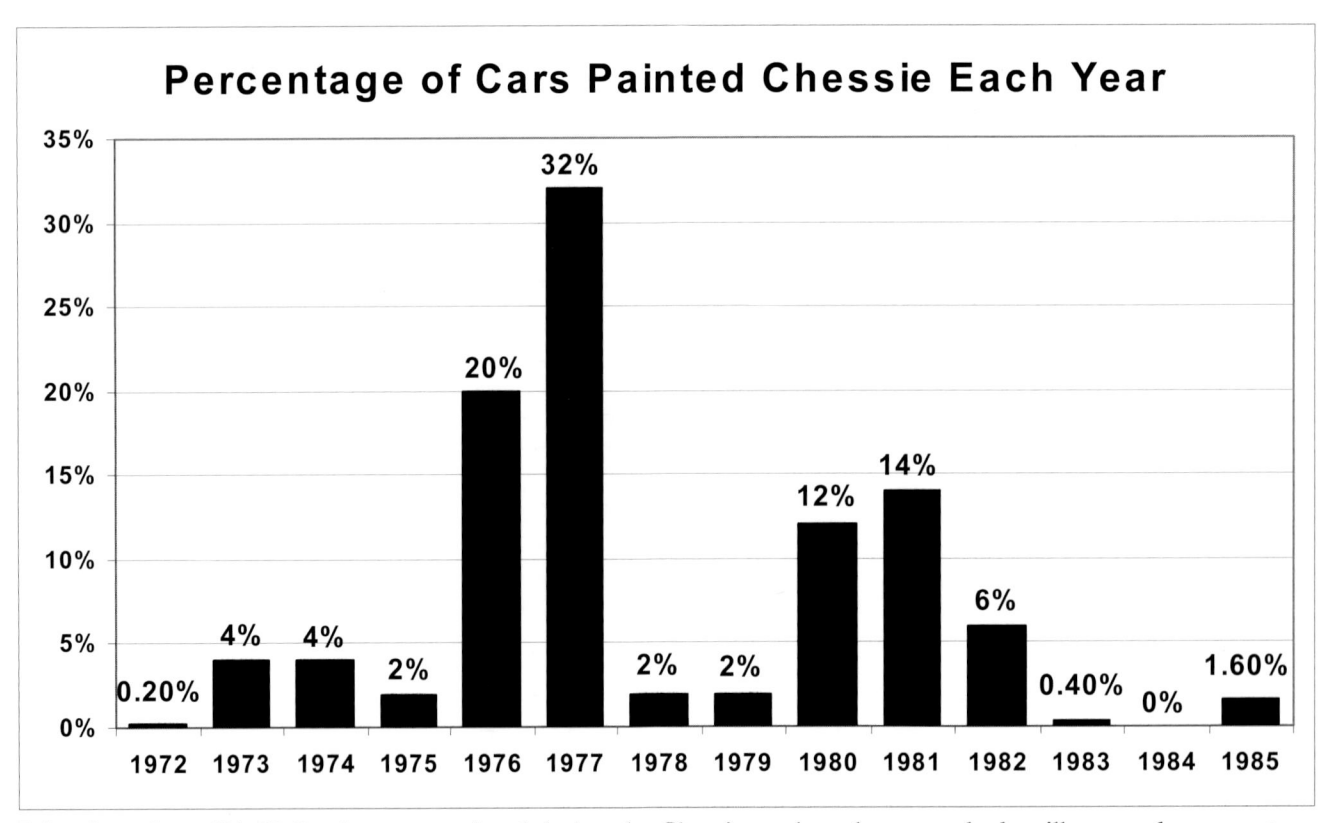

Percentage of Cars Painted Chessie Each Year

Year	Percentage
1972	0.20%
1973	4%
1974	4%
1975	2%
1976	20%
1977	32%
1978	2%
1979	2%
1980	12%
1981	14%
1982	6%
1983	0.40%
1984	0%
1985	1.60%

Paint dates from 484 C&O cabooses repainted during the Chessie era have been graphed to illustrate the percentage of the 484 total that were repainted each year[21] The large number of cabooses repainted in 1976/1977 were mostly class C-25 and C-15C cars completed at Grand Rapids. Those repaintings correspond with the installation of sanitary toilets, as can be seen from studying roster data. The repainting activity in 1980/1981 corresponds with 90200/90300-series cabooses being modernized at Grand Rapids for minerun, terminal, and yard service assignment.

Counting Down the Donuts

Much has been written in the railfan press regarding the last locomotive on CSX still retaining its "C&O" lettering and blue paint. And although it lost its double donut C&O monogram on the ends to CSX yellow, it continued to be a fan favorite right to the very end—it was finally repainted to a full CSX scheme in September 2008. Similarly, a final countdown to the last C&O caboose still retaining its double donut emblem will likely also be of interest to C&O fans.

Beginning our countdown at #3 is C&O 903154, shown at its home terminal at Newark, Ohio, a former B&O yard. The cab was based out of this location for several years, traveling on an assigned run between Newark and Parsons Yard in Columbus. It is shown at Newark on March 17, 2002. It gave up its double donut C&O emblem a few months after this photo was taken when it was repainted into a CSX scheme. CSX later passed this line segment on to a short line, and the 903154 was reassigned to the Cincinnati area, where it still remains in early 2010. *Dwight Jones*

C&O 903238 comes in at #2 in our countdown of remaining cabooses still retaining their double donut C&O emblem. This car had been used by the C&O crew assigned to switch the Ashland Oil refinery complex on the south side of Cattlettsburg, Kentucky. The story on this car was that it reached a state where it was not used by the crew other than as a meeting room. Ashland Oil agreed to construct a building for the crew and the caboose allegedly was "given" to one of the supervisors at Ashland Oil (this was apparently "off the books", as Jacksonville had no knowledge of this). The caboose ended up being shoved to the end of a small dead-end yard. Later a sheet metal building was constructed near the caboose such that the caboose appeared to be land locked. The supervisor that the caboose was "given to" later lost interest in it and the car sat for years in this same location. Some parts even were cannibalized from it. During 2009 a system review of cabooses (shoving platforms) left on CSX resulted in an inspection of this car and a decision to retire it. An investigation of this story resulted in Ashland Oil indicating they had no knowledge of their ownership of this caboose. An historical organization at Cattlettsburg, Kentucky, was given the opportunity to purchase it from CSX and they did.

C&O 903238 departs its longtime storage location near Ashland Oil for its new display site in nearby Cattlettsburg, on May 14, 2010. The author inspected the interior of the cab before loading and was startled by a large snake wrapped around the stove railing. I'm no snake expert, but I think it either was a Boa Constrictor or a Python! *Dwight Jones*

The crew of LR Daniels makes the final adjustment of trucks to place 903238 on its display track adjacent to the Cattlettsburg, Kentucky, C&O depot on May 15, 2010. *Dwight Jones*

Longtime C&O/CSX supervisor Frank Branham, Project Manager for the caboose project, dangles at the photographer a snake skin he found in the caboose. *Dwight Jones*

The Last C&O Caboose

And then there was one. C&O 903305 remains in use by CSX, working out of the former B&O yard at Demmler, Pennsylvania (just east of Pittsburgh). The car is the sole remaining caboose on CSX still wearing its C&O double donut "for progress" emblem and paint scheme. As of 2010 that would be 40 years in the same scheme. And it looks it. As can be seen in this photo showing the car departing Demmler Yard on June 29, 2008, the graffiti artists have tagged this car pretty well. This cab still has most of its original interior accommodations, but these days is used mostly as a shoving platform. What is a shoving platform? It is simply a safe and convenient location where a crew member can position himself to watch the track ahead—exactly the scene that was captured in this photo. Although this car was officially renumbered "90"3305 at Hinton in 1983, that lettering has mostly worn off, exposing its previous number of "C"-3305, which was applied at Hinton in 1979. *Dwight Jones*

Chapter 20

Caboose Trucks

Sometimes, evolution of car components can be as significant as evolution of the car. Trucks, for example, evolved much more than most other major car components. The difference between an archbar truck and its modern descendant is as striking as night and day. Thicker side castings, larger bearing journals, and the introduction of roller bearings were significant advancements in truck design. The photos below are presented to document these changes and furnish modelers with data to ensure model accuracy.

Originally equipped with 5" x 9" journals, A907 had been fitted with trucks having 5" x 8" journals when this photo was made. The two truck sizes were virtually identical, visually. Horizontal braces below the journal housings were eliminated in subsequent years. *Dwight Jones*

Original trucks lasted on caboose A989 right to the end. Note the railway name and journal size cast into the truck frame at lower right. The manufacture date is cast at upper left. *Dwight Jones*

The heritage of C&O caboose 90355 as a Western Maryland car is verified by the WM initials cast in the truck frame at upper left. *Dwight Jones*

131

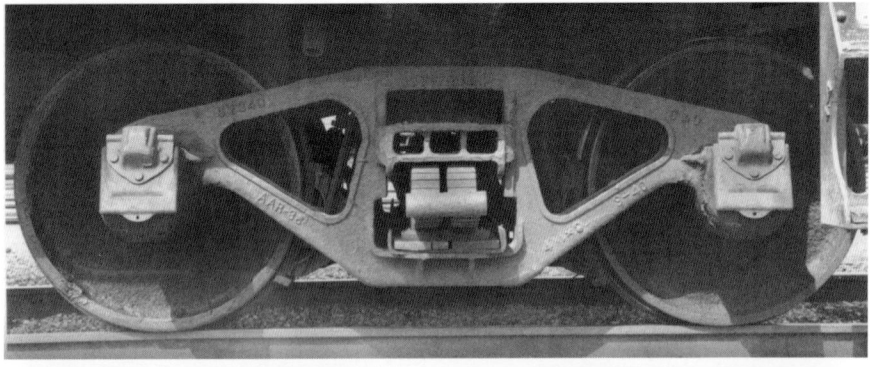

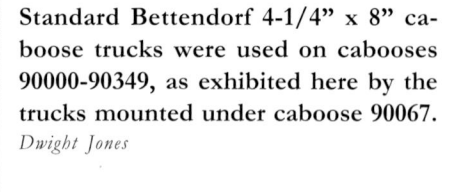

Standard Bettendorf 4-1/4" x 8" caboose trucks were used on cabooses 90000-90349, as exhibited here by the trucks mounted under caboose 90067. *Dwight Jones*

No mistaking these trucks! The Allied Full Cushion truck was synonymous with troop sleepers. The complex design was intended to offer a passenger car-type ride. Most of the former troop sleepers on the C&O used in MofW service and caboose service rode on these trucks. Allied Full Cushion trucks were prohibited in interchange by the Association of American Railroads (AAR), in 1961. *Dwight Jones*

C&O cabooses in series 3100-3325, 3500-3684, and 904094-904159 ride on modern trucks with 5-1/2" x 10" journals equipped with roller bearings, as depicted by these trucks under cab 3514. *Dwight Jones*

When cars undergo heavy repairs, trucks are removed and a careful inspection is made of parts for wear and for cracks or broken parts. Wheels, springs, etc. may need replacement. These three cars were undergoing repair at the Grand Rapids shops on October 9, 1982. Cab 90259 never returned to service—it was sold to a private party. *Dwight Jones*

132 Steel Cabooses of the Chesapeake & Ohio

Axless Trucks

The Differential Steel Car Company (DIFCO) of Findlay, Ohio, is famous for its side dump cars, of which C&O rostered many. Lesser known is the fact that the company experimented with "axless" trucks in the late 1930s and a C&O caboose was involved in the testing, as can be seen from these two DIFCO photos. Steel caboose 90000, C&O's first steel caboose, was virtually brand new when these views were made at the DIFCO plant. Advertised advantages of the design included independent rotation of wheels, mounting of anti-friction bearings in the wheel hub, simplification of truck structure, and single wheel replacement. Apparently nothing ever came of the design. There was no mention of the unique trucks in the 1940 *Car Builders' Cyclopedia*. Caboose 90000 was destroyed in a wreck at Limeville, Kentucky, in 1947, ten years after these photos were made. In the first edition of this book we wondered if the caboose still was wearing the unique trucks when the wreck occurred and if they contributed at all to the derailment.

Fortunately that question now can be answered. Veteran photographer Gene Huddleston visited the derailment site and he advised that standard caboose trucks had been reinstalled on the 90000. Gene also snapped some photos of the incident site, including the view below.[22]

133

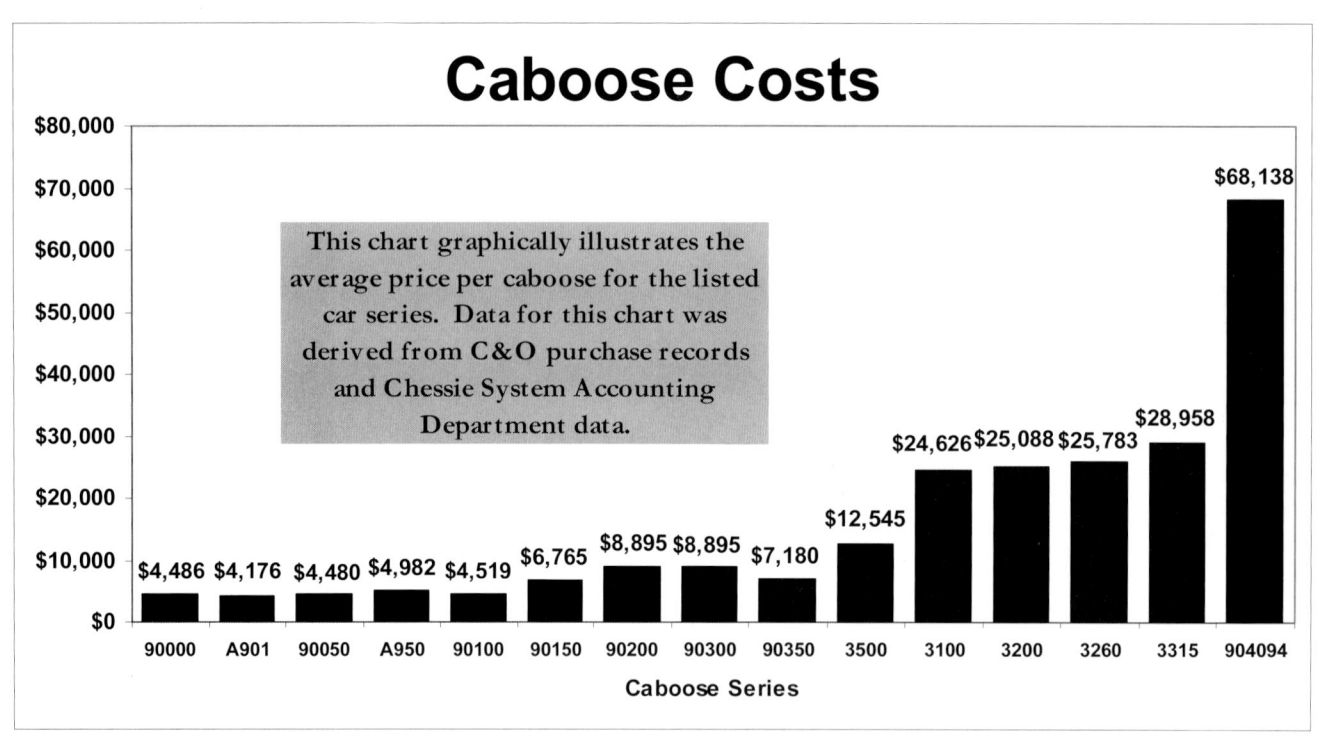

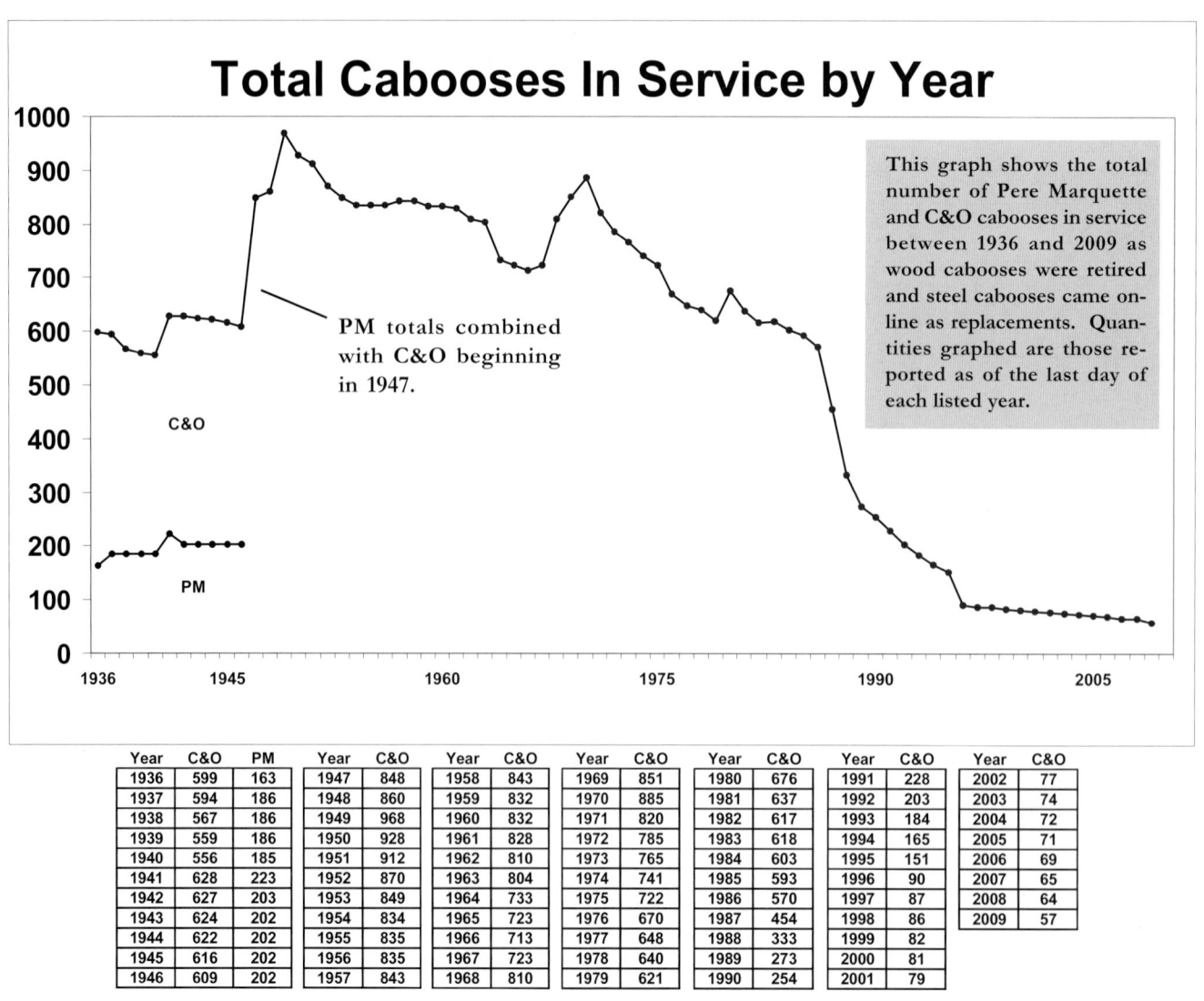

Caboose Costs

This chart graphically illustrates the average price per caboose for the listed car series. Data for this chart was derived from C&O purchase records and Chessie System Accounting Department data.

Caboose Series	Price
90000	$4,486
A901	$4,176
90050	$4,480
A950	$4,982
90100	$4,519
90150	$6,765
90200	$8,895
90300	$8,895
90350	$7,180
3500	$12,545
3100	$24,626
3200	$25,088
3260	$25,783
3315	$28,958
904094	$68,138

Total Cabooses In Service by Year

PM totals combined with C&O beginning in 1947.

This graph shows the total number of Pere Marquette and C&O cabooses in service between 1936 and 2009 as wood cabooses were retired and steel cabooses came on-line as replacements. Quantities graphed are those reported as of the last day of each listed year.

Year	C&O	PM	Year	C&O	Year	C&O	Year	C&O	Year	C&O	Year	C&O	Year	C&O
1936	599	163	1947	848	1958	843	1969	851	1980	676	1991	228	2002	77
1937	594	186	1948	860	1959	832	1970	885	1981	637	1992	203	2003	74
1938	567	186	1949	968	1960	832	1971	820	1982	617	1993	184	2004	72
1939	559	186	1950	928	1961	828	1972	785	1983	618	1994	165	2005	71
1940	556	185	1951	912	1962	810	1973	765	1984	603	1995	151	2006	69
1941	628	223	1952	870	1963	804	1974	741	1985	593	1996	90	2007	65
1942	627	203	1953	849	1964	733	1975	722	1986	570	1997	87	2008	64
1943	624	202	1954	834	1965	723	1976	670	1987	454	1998	86	2009	57
1944	622	202	1955	835	1966	713	1977	648	1988	333	1999	82		
1945	616	202	1956	835	1967	723	1978	640	1989	273	2000	81		
1946	609	202	1957	843	1968	810	1979	621	1990	254	2001	79		

Chapter 21

Caboose Markers

Caboose markers have evolved over the years from the large kerosene markers that date to early in the 20th Century to the economical and simple markers of the 1960s. Kerosene, electrical and reflectorized caboose markers have become collectibles in the railroadiana market. The ones in this chapter are samples from the author's collection.

At the start of the steel-caboose era, black kerosene markers were the standard on both the C&O and Pere Marquette. The color of C&O markers was changed to yellow at some point, although PM markers remained black. C&O markers used one red and three yellow lenses. When not in use, kerosene markers were stored inside the caboose, hanging on a pair of caboose marker light brackets. These high-maintenance lights required replacement wicks and kerosene, and had to be lit when required.

Kerosene markers typically had permanent identification listing the railroad name. This could have been in the form of a metal tag attached to the light or the initials stamped into the sides of the marker.

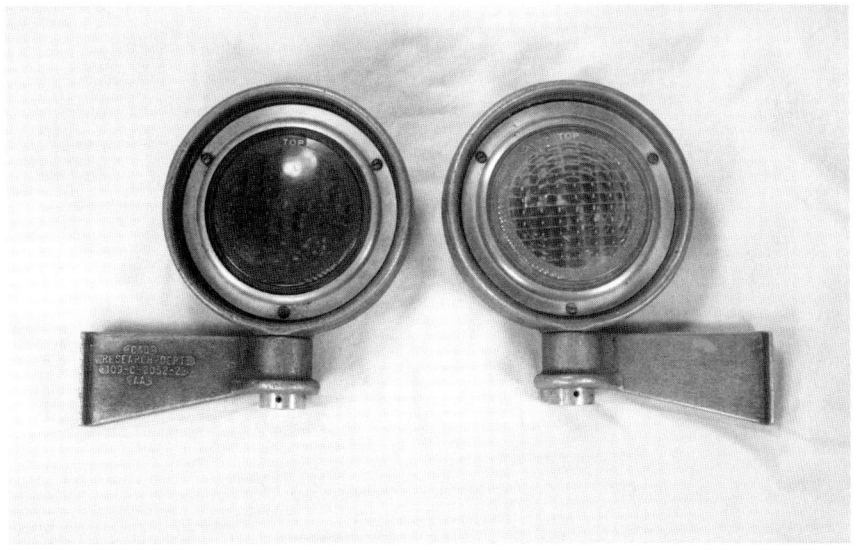

Around 1954 the C&O Research Department designed these markers as a cost-effective replacement for kerosene markers. The markers are almost always shown on the rear of C&O Roadrailer cars and they may have been designed for that service. The circular reflector could be rotated in the arm. Colors were red on one side and yellow on the opposite side. Photos do show an occasional caboose application. We wonder where these lights were stored when not in use. Perhaps a car department employee removed and stored them. The circular part of the caboose marker measured seven inches in diameter.

135

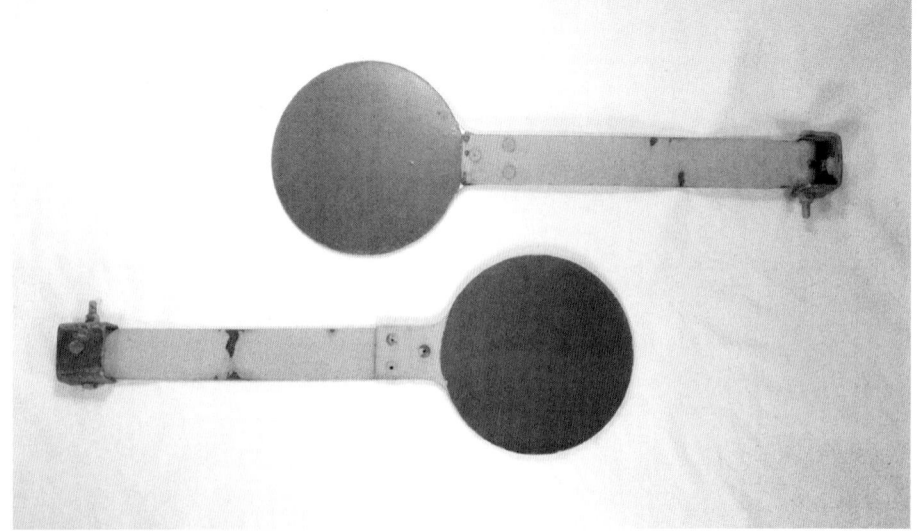

As the kerosene markers became more expensive, many railroads opted for a less expensive alternative, both in original cost and in on-going maintenance. These paddle type markers were unique to the **C&O** and from their construction appear to have been made in the railroad's own shops, probably Huntington. The paddles could be both retracted and rotated to display the opposite side. Typical **C&O** marker colors appeared using reflectorized material—yellow on one side and red on the opposite. The circular part measured six inches in diameter. C&O drawing 154-4-431 documented the application of these markers to cabooses and is dated 5-28-64. Photos show the markers on cabooses by October 1964. Some C&O employees indicate these were known as "lolly pops".

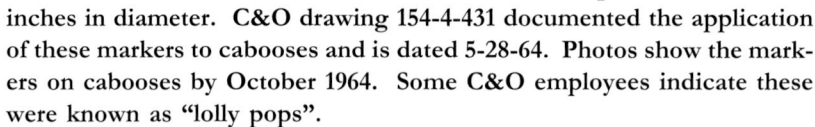

A close-up look at a midget electric marker light manufactured by Pyle National. This one is on one of the very early 3500-series cabs before release to service at the Grand Rapids shops in early 1969. Note that a piece of metal has been welded across the top of the attachment bracket to prevent the marker from being removed from the caboose. To change the bulb, the knurled screw on the top could be unthreaded and the top of the marker removed. A chain kept the top attached to the base. If the color of the lens needed to be changed, the top could be rotated left or right. These markers measured approximately 5" high with 1-1/2" diameter lenses. Whether it was kerosene markers, midget electric markers, or the later box style shown below, C&O specified a red lens to the rear, with all other lenses being yellow.

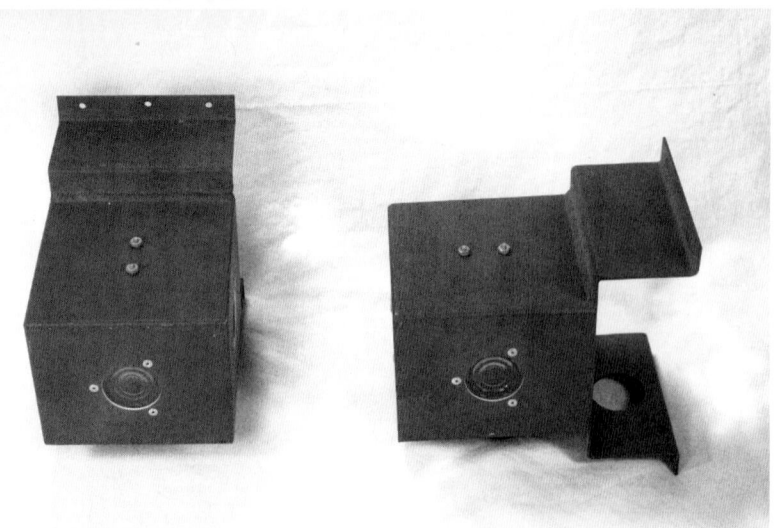

Electric box marker lights first appeared on new **B&O** cabooses in 1975 and continued on other batches of new cabs purchased in 1978 and 1980. They also were retrofitted to cabooses already in service on all three Chessie component roads. The retrofit lights, shown here, contained brackets that allowed them to be placed over and straddle the existing marker light attachment brackets. The new box lights then were welded to the body sides or attached with pop rivets. These box lights were 4" high and contained 1-1/2" diameter lenses. This pair of lights, presented to the author by a car foreman from their stock, were never installed on a caboose and are in red oxide primer paint. It was not unusual to see primer painted markers on in-service cabooses. These lights had two advantages over the midget electric markers. One, they were permanently mounted to the caboose and could not be removed by "collectors". And secondly, the bottom side of the box was a hinged piece of plexiglass, needed for access to the bulb, but also supplying downward light that would help highlight the side grabiron and step locations at night.

136   Steel Cabooses of the Chesapeake & Ohio

This close-up view shows the application of the newer style box markers to an older caboose which originally had one of the midget electric markers. The box marker straddles the original marker light bracket, which still is attached to the side of the caboose. This particular box marker is one wearing only iron oxide primer. Notice that this box marker has been attached with pop rivets, which was the standard application according to Mechanical Department specifications. Some cars, however, had their straddle brackets welded to the side of the caboose. Photographed on caboose 903163 at Bad Axe, Michigan on October 9, 1982. *Dwight Jones*

This Chessie System drawing of the new box markers was prepared in April 1979 and carries a note that it was based on a similar drawing from International Car Corporation. These style markers debuted in 1978 on a batch of new B&O bay-window cabooses from International Car.

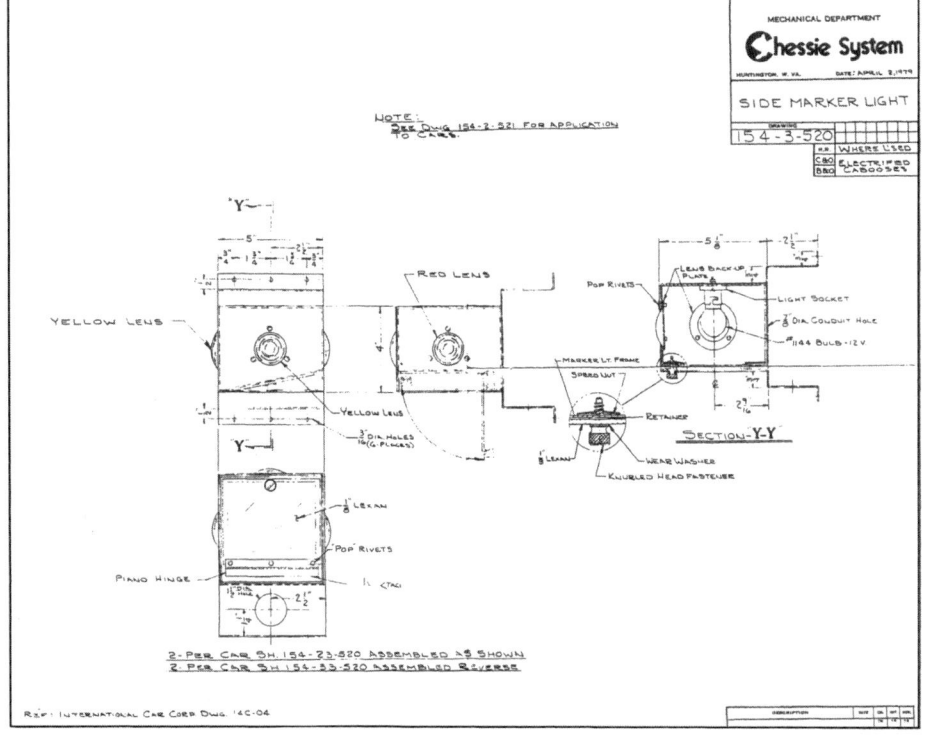

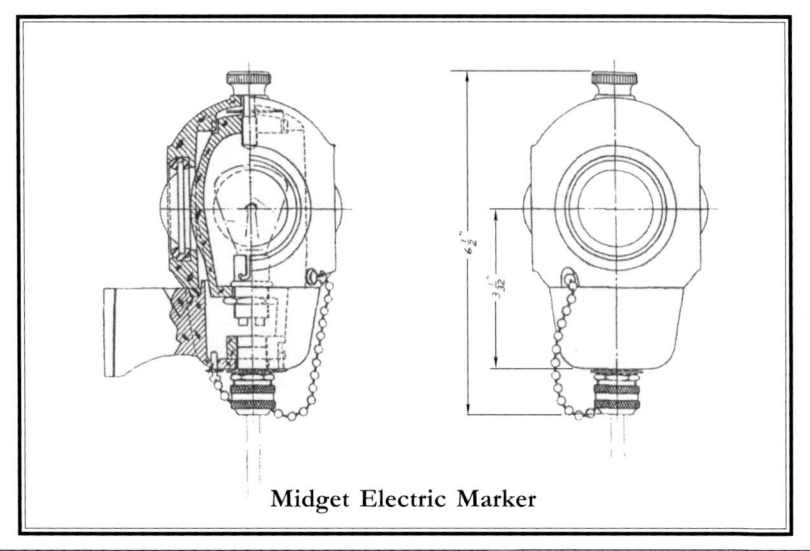

This drawing of the midget electric marker lights provides a look at the inside workings of the unit, showing the bulb and the knurled nut on the top.

Midget Electric Marker

137

An interesting night photo probably shot at Huntington in the late 1950s/early 1960s showing bright markers. The visible kerosene marker does not appear to have a chimney cap.
C&OHS collection

Note that both of these first-generation steel cabooses have wood end platforms at this era.

Below, a trainman is demonstrating the correct way to attach a rear marker—feet apart, left hand firmly grasping the vertical handhold. These markers were heavy, weighing over 10 pounds. This training photo was likely made at Saginaw in November 1946.
C&OHS collection

C&O rule books and employee timetables of the late 1950s and early 1960s make reference to "Reflex Markers" and permitting their use. We have not found clarification on exactly what these were but the word reflex is similar to reflective and possibly could be the name for the round reflective markers which are documented in the third photo of this chapter and which were used on Roadrailer equipment with some limited caboose application.

138   Steel Cabooses of the Chesapeake & Ohio

Notes

1. Using the "in service" data from the rosters, the following is a geographical breakdown of those cabooses considered "active" in 1983:

Michigan	24%
West Virginia	23%
Kentucky	20%
Ohio	14%
Virginia	13%
Canada	3%
Illinois	2%
Indiana	1%

2. Location of ladders on certain PM/C&O steel cabooses has been somewhat baffling. With the exception of the C&O 90300-series cabooses (which were for service on the PM District), C&O steel cabooses have consistently had ladders located on the right side of the end. Older PM wooden cabooses appear to have also been consistent with respect to ladder placement on the right side. Why, then, did PM deviate and specify ladders on the left side of their last wood-sheathed cabooses (A800 series)? The A901 series cabs were delivered with end ladders moved back to the right side. Then the A950 series cabooses were delivered with ladders on the left side. The 90300 series PM District cars also came with end ladders on the left side.

3. Wayner Publications, *The Complete Roster of Heavyweight Pullman Cars* (New York, 1985), page 253.

4. War Assets Administration (WAA) was the government agency established to dispose of excess government-owned material at the conclusion of World War II. C&O car records indicate the original road number on troop cars that were acquired by C&O as "WAA number". That designation has been maintained in this book, although it is doubtful the cars ever actually carried "WAA" reporting marks.

5. Imagine my surprise, when reviewing C&O car records at the Operating Headquarters building at Huntington in late 1984, to find noted on the record card for X1183 that it had been sold to the B&O Museum. I had never seen any C&O troop cars at the museum or stored in the back lot. A call to museum officials confirmed that they knew nothing of the car either. In mid-1985, while in Baltimore on a research trip, I was able to check some supplemental records in downtown offices and uncovered some additional information. In late 1976 C&O Authorization for Expenditure (AFE) 29175 had been issued to transfer ownership of X1183 from C&O to B&O. B&O AFE 56772 then was issued to transfer ownership to the B&O Museum account (as we understood it, C&O could not directly transfer equipment to the B&O Museum). C&O X1183 was indeed being carried on the museum's account. Armed with this additional information, I again approached museum officials. Glad to get these new findings, museum officials contacted the Mechanical Department in Huntington at the OH Building and a system-wide check was made to locate the missing car. Alas, the car could not be located. As the story unfolded, the Mechanical Department suggested that a Western Maryland troop car be substituted, number 911921. That car had been placed into Dismantle category at Cumberland on June 6, 1985. It had been renumbered from Western Maryland B3002 at Cumberland on June 26, 1982, and was carried as a sleeper with a 5-47 build date (more likely a conversion date) in nonrevenue car records. A check of my photos showed that the candidate still had all side windows intact, still rode on Allied Full Cushion trucks, and was in the WM's red oxide camp car scheme. The WM car now resides at the museum.

6. Although a photo of a C&O Troop Sleeper caboose has yet to surface, a first hand account was provided to us by retired C&O employee Frank Branham who remembers one operating out of the 34th Street Yard at Ashland, Kentucky, on the Mill Job. He reports the car was painted caboose red and had white lettering with "Chesapeake & Ohio" spelled out on the side. The era was 1948-49.

7. Throughout this book there has been no mention of the financing arrangements under which C&O and PM acquired caboose cars. Seldom were cars purchased outright, except, for instance, in the case of acquisitions of secondhand cars such as the 90350 series WM cabs. First-generation C&O and PM cabooses were financed using equipment trusts. Data to that effect was stenciled in the upper left corner on the side of each caboose, as can be seen from examining builder's photos in this book. In later years C&O/B&O used a variety of financing methods to acquire caboose cars, such as CSA's (Conditional Sale Agreements), leases, and equipment trusts. No matter the financing medium, when it was completed, the stenciling on each car would be painted over.

8. The July 1, 1972, date that we have provided for banning the Duryea underframe in interchange service was taken from the 1970 edition of the AAR Interchange Rules.

9. For more information on the Reading-style caboose, see the three-part series that appeared in *Railroad Model Craftsman*, July, August, and September 1982 issues.

10. A number of different terms have been used to describe cabooses whose cupolas are wider than the main body. Some have used the term "extended vision", while Car Cyclopedias called them "wide vision". International Car called them "extra wide vision" while others have referred to them as "saddle bag" cupola cabooses.

11. The original roof color specified on painting and lettering drawing 152-6-1053 was gray. Roof color was changed to blue with a drawing revision dated 12-20-68. When the C&O photographer visited Grand Rapids around January 1969, he photographed all of the early rebuilds that still were at the shops. His photos show those early rebuilds as having gray roofs, but in-service photos of these same cars taken later show blue roofs, leading to our speculation that those early cars had their roofs repainted blue before initial release from the shops.

12. Certain C-15C cars have steel plates welded to the left of the doors to seal a window opening. Interesting is the fact that cars in series 90000-90199, from which the C-15C cars were rebuilt, originally had end windows only to the right of the door. In reexamining older photos of cars in series 90000-90199, we did locate a couple that showed windows on the left side of the door. We have no additional data to explain why windows in those first-generation cabooses were changed.

13. C&O/Carl W. Shaver, *Freight Car Equipment of the Chesapeake & Ohio Railway*, August 1, 1937, (Alderson, 1980), plate B-6.

14. When we received Chessie's diagram sheet for the former Toledo Terminal cabooses, in February 1986, we were surprised to see that all four cabooses were shown on the same diagram sheet as class C-29. We have elected to show only the three cars that actually match the diagram. For the trivia buffs, this was the first caboose diagram sheet to be made on Chessie's new computer-aided drawing system.

15. Some of the more interesting paint variations we have seen and photographed during the Chessie years include the B&O GP9 with the "B&O for Progress" lettering, the locomotive delivered new from General Electric and lettered "hessie System" on one side, the B&O covered hopper lettered "Chsiees Syemst", the GE locomotive painted at Huntington shops and lettered "Chess e System", the B&O and C&O hopper cars with unorthodox Chess-C emblems, the B&O box car lettered "Chsiees Syemst" . . .

16. The examples listed are not based on analysis of a few random cabooses. We have examined and photographed each of the cabooses carried on the C&O/B&O/WM caboose roster. Well over 1000 cars.

17. To examine paint and lettering data properly, a number of sources should be used and carefully analyzed. Included are paint and lettering drawings, painting specifications, photos and personal observations. There are good and bad attributes of each of the listed sources, and those must also be taken into account during the analysis process. Suffice it to say that we are aware of those pitfalls and have tried to take them into account in our analysis.

18. One additional explanations for blue cabooses are advanced here. B&O began painting cabooses blue (with yellow ends) in 1965 to signify a car qualified for system pool service. Some have felt that the introduction of blue for C&O/B&O cabooses in 1968 was, therefore, merely an extension of the B&O practice. It is clear that on the C&O a blue caboose signified a car that likewise was qualified for divisional pool requirements. A C&O memo indicated that blue cabooses were "suitable for mainline service" and that yellow cabooses were "suitable primarily for yard, shifter and transfer service".

19. If you are wondering, as we did, about the background story to the N&W adopting blue as their caboose color, Arthur M. Bixby, Sr., Historian for the Roanoke Chapter of the National Railway Historical Society, explained to us in an April 11, 1968, letter that the color was a matter of presidential preference. Bixby further explained that when Stuart Saunders left the N&W in June 1963, he was succeeded by Herman Pevler, who came from the Wabash Railroad, and, naturally, he favored the "Wabash Blue" for caboose cars. The blue was adopted on N&W about 1965-66 after merger of the Wabash and several other railroads into the N&W in 1964. Bixby also wrote that "Herman Pevler was a strong willed individual, whom I knew for many years, when he was with the Pennsylvania Railroad as a Vice President in New York, prior to joining the Wabash. In my estimation, he wished to perpetuate the Wabash Blue color on the N&W, when he had the authority to do so."

20. Throughout this book we have tried to emphasize that painting and lettering deviations were many and, quite often, difficult to categorize. An additional one that deserves mention is the metal window awnings over the caboose side windows. Several color photos taken in the 1950s, including this book's cover photo, show these awnings painted black, although there is no notation to that effect on any company documents that we have examined.

21. As stated in the Roster Interpretation section, Chessie did not keep records of caboose paint dates. The ones we charted were copied directly from the side of the cabooses. Some cars had repaint dates but no shop code. In a very few cases, some cars for which data was extracted were in their second Chessie coat, and the first repaint data was, unfortunately, not obtained. In other cases no information could be obtained from the side of the caboose, owing either to the fact that it had not been originally stenciled, or it had been removed by chemical washings. That is why the total car quantities differ between Figure 1 and Figure 2. We do feel that the charted data is extremely accurate even with the omissions described.

22. After publication of the first edition of this book, retired Ohio Division Superintendent of Operations John Riddle, who worked his entire life for the C&O, wrote to say this about the wrecked 90000 at Limeville. "I was on that caboose before its removal from the accident site. It was on the west end of a train in No.3 setoff track at NJ Cabin (Limeville) and was struck by engine 2705 moving eastward. My memory of the accident tells me that it occurred in a dense fog. I can assure you that it was not on axless trucks, therefore they were not a factor in the accident. The cast number plate on the smokebox of the 2705 was destroyed in the accident and was replaced with one made of steel plate."

23. Photographer Fellure indicated that this display also included GP30 3028 in the "new" Enchantment Blue" scheme with big block C&O initials. The two models, both secretaries in the Mechanical Department, were Connie Wilson on the end platform and Lana Rood.

Caboose Markings of the Modern Era

ACI Plate
Automatic Car Identification plate, 10-1/2" wide x 22" high black plate with multicolored stripes which could be read by a line-side scanner to identify car number and reporting marks. The ACI plate applications were made per the requirements of AAR bulletin 40622 which was dated November 22, 1967. This new identification program was intended to be a tremendous advantage to the railroad industry. Each piece of rolling stock was to have its own unique ACI label which could be read by a scanner as the car rolled by. The plan was to have these scanners located at key yards where arrivals and departures could be recorded, thus eliminating the need for a clerk to manually do this chore. The system was relatively short-lived. In 1977 the Association of American Railroads issued a report outlining why the 10-year, $150 million program might be abandoned. There were a number of problems with the system including the fact that all railroads did not embrace the system, and that the line-side scanners were not 100% effective. In late 1977, a 5-1 AAR vote ended the program.

Consolidated Stencil
The Federal Railroad Administration mandated that all cars be equipped with consolidated stencils beginning July 1, 1974, with all cars to be so stencilled by January 1, 1979. The purpose of the consolidated stencil, as its name implies, is to consolidate in one convenient location, car data previously stencilled at other locations, including air reservoirs and car sides. Over the years the size and dimensions of the stencil have evolved; currently a single block is used. Stencilled information includes date built and/or rebuilt, recondition date, lube data, inspection information, and brake maintenance data.

Wheel Inspection Symbol
This symbol was a 12" square black block with a 6" colored dot applied in the center. A rash of derailments across the US in 1977/78 were traced to a Southern U-1 wheel manufactured by the Abex Manufacturing Company (or a predecessor company) between 1958 and 1969. These wheels were found to heat up and crack under pressure. The 33" diameter wheels were recalled by the FRA. Effective April 1, 1978, railroads were to inspect equipment for these wheels and use a yellow dot to indicate no such wheels were on the car, or a white dot to indicate the car did have the suspect wheels. Cars with white dots were restricted from trains carrying hazardous materials. The program apparently was to continue until all 100,000 suspect wheels were purged from the US fleet.

C&O/B&O/WM
Caboose Summary 1987, 2010

SERIES	RR	CLASS	DATE BUILT	BUILT BY	TYPE	ORIGINALLY BUILT	ON ROSTER Jan 1987	ON ROSTER Jan 2010
900050-900199	C&O	C-15A	1941-47	Note 1	Cupola	150	1	0
900200-900299	C&O	C-20	1949	AC&F	Cupola	100	74	0
900300-900349	C&O	C-21	1949	AC&F	Cupola	50	34	0
900350-900356	C&O	C-13	1936-40	BS-WM	Cupola	7	2	0
900901-900925	C&O	C-14	1937	Magor	Cupola	25	1	0
900950-900989	C&O	C-16	1941	SLC	Cupola	40	12	0
903100-903325	C&O	C-25	1968-71	ICC	Cupola	226	219	29
903326	C&O	C-29	1945	LV	Cupola	1	1	0
903327-903329	C&O	C-29	1950	ICC	Cupola	3	3	0
903500-903684	C&O	C-15C	1937-47	Note 1	Cupola	185	173	0
904094-904159	C&O	C-27A	1980	FGE	Baywindow	66	65	28
							Total	57
902400-902499	B&O	C-18	1941-42	B&O	Baywindow	100	14	0
902800-902824	B&O	C-18	1945	B&O	Baywindow	25	9	0
902850-902861	B&O	C-22	1952-53	B&O	Baywindow	12	6	0
902862-902909	B&O	C-23	1953-58	B&O	Baywindow	48	21	0
902925-902960	B&O	C-23	1959-1965	B&O	Baywindow	36	14	0
903000-903045	B&O	C-24	1965-66	ICC	Baywindow	46	41	4
903050	B&O	C-15B	1941	Magor	Cupola	1	1	0
903051	B&O	C-28	1952/1976	Note 2	Transfer	1	0	0
903700-903827	B&O	C-26	1971	ICC	Baywindow	128	53	1
903828-903924	B&O	C-26A	1975	ICC	Baywindow	97	95	25
903925-903986	B&O	C-27	1978	FGE	Baywindow	62	61	21
904000-904093	B&O	C-27A	1980	FGE	Baywindow	94	94	44
							Total	95
901801-901905	WM	C-13A	1936-40	BS-WM	Cupola	105	53	0

Builder Codes:

Note 1: 3 lots, built by AC&F, SLC and Magor (C-15C cars rebuilt from C-15 and C-15A cars by C&O)
Note 2: built by Pullman Standard as a boxcar; rebuilt by B&O Du Bois shops as a caboose
AC&F American Car & Foundry
BS-WM Bethlehem Steel kits assembled by Western Maryland
Magor Magor Car Corporation
SLC St. Louis Car Company
ICC International Car Company
FGE Fruit Growers Express
B&O Various B&O shops
LV Lehigh Valley

Note: Some cars shown as on the roster in January 2010 now wear a number in the CSX shoving platform series.

Acknowledgments

First Edition

Certainly no book of this kind can be completed without a lot of help. A whole host of individuals both in and out of the railroad profession have contributed their individual knowledge for the collective good of this work.

From the C&O Historical Society a number of members and officers gave freely of their time, data, and photos. Carl Shaver, who originated the idea for the first edition of this book, had already recorded much C&O caboose history in the form of his monthly caboose column in The C&O Historical Newsletter. In addition, he reviewed the final draft and made many valuable comments. Tom Dixon enthusiastically approved this project, kept our nose to the grindstone on the original version, and supplied material from the C&OHS collection as well as material from his personal collection. Bob Michaels, in addition to reviewing the original draft copies we sent him, furnished valuable data from his extensive personal records and kept us abreast of new developments from his research trips across the system. The late Art Million, long recognized as a Pere Marquette authority, checked our PM chapters and data and gave much appreciated help and suggestions. Other C&OHS members who helped were Dick Argo, James EuDaly, Paul Dunn, Gene Huddleston, Jim Lindholm, Tom Lindholm, Larry McNutt and Ted Wetterstroem.

Perhaps unique among historical societies is the relationship that existed between the C&O Historical Society and Chessie System Railroads. During the five years that the first edition of this book was in work, we talked to dozens of Chessie employees across all parts of the system. Almost to a person, all took time from their busy schedules to grant permissions, or answer questions, give permission for photos to be taken, allow documents to be copied, or at least provide a lead or two for additional information. Many of these people have since become cherished friends that we continue to work with on future projects. Certainly a big tip of the hat is due from all of us in the historical community to the following Chessie men and women: George Athanas, Curtis Barr, Gary Brannock, Jim Burnette, Teddy Cain, Franklyn Carr, J.J. Cassidy, Brian Clark, Henry DeVries, Frank Dewey, Ron Drucker, John Eccleston, Andy Foster, Danny Friedman, Carol Geben, Art Gladstone, H.J. Harbert, Crew Heimer, George Hendrien, Bucky Jones, Chuck Jones, Lloyd Lewis, Frank LeMaster, Mike Martino, Charlie Mewshaw, Jack Mills, Kenny Morriss, Billy Jack Peirce, Bob Perkins, Delse Piper, Dennis Richmond, John Riddle, Jim Sadler, John Shanahan, Ora Sheets, Maurice Short, Larry Smith, Jack Spatig, Jim Spainhower, Steve Tackett, W. B. Vander Veer, Jerry Wess, Harry White and Al Wiles.

In addition to those Chessie people listed, there were many others whose names, regrettably, we did not get. These included yardmasters, clerks, car department people, trainmasters and the like who we came across in our travels across the railroad. To those we offer our apologies. And to all who helped a big THANK YOU!

2010 Edition

During four research trips to the Clifton Forge archives new information was uncovered thanks to Rick Traab, Tom Dixon, Lars Lemberg, and particularly to Mac Beard, who scanned many documents and photos for us. Ed Allen also provided photo scanning help. A number of knowledgeable fans helped by reviewing the manuscript and offering suggestions including David Jones, Ed Kirstatter, Phil Shuster, and Everett Young. Special thanks is due Carl Shaver our Editor-in-Chief, with his box of colons, comas, hyphens, indentations and em dashes. He is also a subject matter expert.

Many thanks is also due to our many CSX friends, particularly our good friend Mike Montonera. Other key contacts who helped include Joseph Brinker, Jim Briskey, Roger Eastham, Everett Eddy, Richard Godby, Danny Greer, Jeff Hensley, Dale Johnson, Bart, Kohl, Scott Marshall, Charlie Miller, Mike Mitchell, Rami Rawda, Alan Smith, Len Whitehead and Rick Wilson.

Before we extinguish the flame in the ol' kerosene caboose lamp, we will ask for your help. If you discover any errors in this book, or have any additional information on any part of this book, we would like to hear from you.

Dwight Jones
536 Clairbrook Avenue
Columbus, Ohio 43228

614-870-7315
email: csxcabooses@msn.com

Want More Information?

A book such as this provides only a brief mention of the history of the cabooses covered. The references below are recommended reading for additional data on cabooses and are by this same author.

Steel Cabooses of the Chesapeake & Ohio, 1937-1987, is a 122-page soft cover book published in 1987 by the C&O Historical Society. This book covers the complete history of the steel caboose fleet of the C&O, including heavy photo coverage, diagram sheets, full rosters by individual car number, and related material. One of the first books published on the history of cabooses of a specific railroad, it now is out of print. The original version can still be found at on-line auctions, used book sources, and at railroad shows. The book you now are reading is the second edition of this book, with expanded coverage of these C&O cabooses.

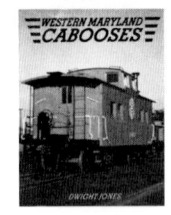

Western Maryland Cabooses, published in 1991 by the Western Maryland Railway Historical Society and available in both soft and hard cover versions, is a 194-page publication covering the caboose fleet of this popular eastern railroad. From bobber cabooses to troop sleeper cabs to the steel caboose fleet built in the late 1930s and early 1940s, this book covers the entire history of the cabooses of this interesting railroad. Extensive photo coverage, including a color section, full roster for the steel cars, and detailed historical text all combine to make this one of the most extensive caboose histories ever published. Order from Western Maryland Railway Historical Society, Box 395, Union Bridge, MD 21791.

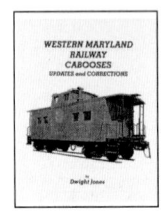

Western Maryland Cabooses, updates and corrections, published in 2003 by the Western Maryland Railway Historical Society, P.O. Box 395, Union Bridge, MD 21791, is a 44 page soft-cover publication providing updated information as well as corrections for the book *Western Maryland Cabooses* listed above. This publication is loaded with photos and updated disposition information for the Western Maryland's steel cabooses and troop sleepers. The original book was published in 1991. This update brings the reader new information not available for inclusion in the original book. Available from the Western Maryland Railway Historical Society.

Chesapeake & Ohio Cabooses, 90700 Series, is a 50-page soft cover book covering the full history of the 100 cabooses in this interesting C&O wood caboose series. Caboose historians Dwight Jones and Phil Samuell teamed up to produce this extremely detailed work on these cars built in 1924. This book includes extensive photo coverage of in-service cars, as well as cars owned by private owners. Included is a complete roster by individual car number. Step-by-step refurbishment of one of the cars will be of interest to anyone restoring a caboose. This is the only book that covers the detailed history of wood C&O cabooses. Available ($14 postpaid) from Dwight Jones, address on the previous page.

B&O Cabooses, Photos and Diagrams, was published in 1998 by TLC Publishing, 1387 Winding Creek Lane, Lynchburg, VA 24503. This 124-page hard cover book provides an overview of the entire B&O caboose fleet from the late 1800s to 1980, including extensive coverage with photos and diagrams. Over 30 years of meticulous research has gone into this volume. It is the most accurate publication on B&O cabooses ever produced, correcting many errors already in circulation. This book is the only complete reference for B&O caboose diagrams.

C&O/B&O Cabooses, Display and Private Owner Cars, Volume I, II, III contains photo and history coverage of approximately 550 C&O and B&O cabooses sold by the railroad and now on display in city parks, in backyards, in museums, on tourist railroads, etc. Additional sections provide coverage on moving a caboose, caboose trains operated by shortline and tourist railroads, and more. Softcover, with color covers. Available directly from the author, volume I =$15.95; volume II = $16.95; volume III = $17.95 + 3.50 S/H: Dwight Jones, 536 Clairbrook Avenue, Columbus, Ohio 43228.

For serious students of C&O and B&O cabooses, as well as other equipment historians, a detailed listing of display and private owner car photos appearing in all of our publications will be of interest. This listing details over 700 line items of caboose photos appearing in all of the books listed on this page. The files are produced using Word and Excel programs. Available for $5.00, which includes postage, directly from the author.

Want More Information?

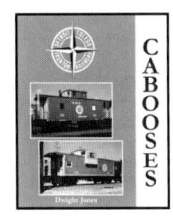

DT&I Cabooses, is a 96-page softcover book covering cabooses of the Detroit, Toledo and Ironton Railroad, from the earliest wood four-wheel cabooses and boxcar conversions, up through the steel cupola cars, which were both purchased new by the DT&I and acquired secondhand from other lines. This book is heavy on photo coverage, and includes a complete roster of all steel cabooses as well as the 40 wood cars purchased during the time Henry Ford owned the DT&I. Color photos illustrate paint and lettering schemes. Each of the steel DT&I cabooses is shown. Dwight Jones, 536 Clairbrook Avenue, Columbus, Ohio 43228. ($29.99 plus $4 shipping, plus $2 OH residents state tax)

We ran out of room in the above book for all of the information that we wanted to present on the subject of DT&I cabooses. This supplement will contain copies of official DT&I diagram sheets for the cabooses, official DT&I investigation/hearing where a caboose was damaged, index of photos in the book, interior photos of caboose 116, interior photos of wood caboose 77, listing of cabooses in service by year from the 1920s to the retirement of the last caboose, additional wood caboose paint dates, and more. *Available after August 2010.*

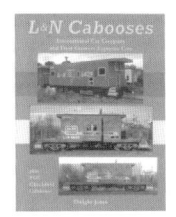

L&N Cabooses, International Car and Fruit Growers Express Cars, is a 96 page soft cover book covering the full history of these 100 cabooses, which were the last cabooses purchased new by the Louisville & Nashville. The book is heavy on photos and presents a photo of each of the 100 L&N cabooses covered as well as an additional 6 FGE cabooses purchased for the Clinchfield. Photo coverage includes over 200 black-and-white photos and 23 color images, as well as several charts, graphs and diagrams. A complete roster by individual caboose number is included, giving final disposition data. ($29.99 plus $4 shipping & $2 OH residents state tax.)

Still to Come ...

Wanted

The author is always looking for B&O caboose photos and slides showing cars wearing pre-Chessie System paint schemes.

The C&O used a number of smaller shops to perform repairs and repainting to locally-assigned cabooses. These four cars had just been completed in the roundhouse at Walbridge. Photographed on April 4, 1963, from left to right are shown wood 90957 and 90782, then A917 and A916. It is likely that some or all of these cars had been in the red scheme prior to this shopping. *Kirk Hise*

C&O Cabooses In Color!

Caboose 90184 is shown at Russell, probably in early 1954, after being painted at the Russell shops in December 1953 with Sherwin-Williams paint. Note the application of metallic brown to the steps. *C&OHS collection*

Pere Marquette A918 was photographed at Plymouth, Michigan, in January 1962. It last had been painted at Saginaw in 1957. This is a rare photo of a steel caboose in red paint with the new 1954 emblem. An odd electric cord extends from the left window implying something electrical inside. Veteran C&O employee Phil Shuster comments that trainmen frequently carried coffee makers, hot plates, and electric fry pans for their creature comforts. In order to use these they had to plug into a trackside source of electric power. Most employees had 100 foot long extension cords in their caboose lockers and they would have their cab spotted as close as possible to such a source. Note that a kerosene lamp shows in the right window. *Emory Gulash*

The conductor on #93 reaches to grab the orders at Muncie, Indiana, on September 5, 1955. He already has tossed the waybills, which show as the white papers in midair just under the orders hoop. Caboose 90288 wears a nice pair of yellow kerosene marker lights. Note the light mounted to the top of the pole which is holding the orders hoop. It must have been a real challenge to grab the orders after dark. The rear flagman has the easy job. *James F. EuDaly*

C&O 90323 is shown on a shop track at an unidentified location in the early 1950s. Given that the 90300s were purchased for service on the Pere Marquette District, and the trucks were not painted (a requirement of the PM District painting specification), the photo likely was made at a C&O shop in Michigan. *C&OHS collection*

What is believed to be the very first C&O caboose to be painted in the yellow paint scheme was on display at Richmond, Virginia, for the 1956 Stockholderama. A black-and-white photo was used in the first edition of this book (see the painting chapter) but now this color view of the opposite side has been uncovered at the C&OHS Archives. This view presents the new information of the red safety appliances and confirms the different lettering style on this side. Below left, the 90001 is shown back in service on the Hocking Division, probably around 1958. Note that the red safety railings which were exhibited at Richmond now have been changed to green, although the two different lettering versions were retained. *Above, C&OHS Archives, left, Dick Argo*

148   Steel Cabooses of the Chesapeake & Ohio

Caboose A971 was in relatively fresh paint when photographed in 1960 at Ionia, Michigan. This view presents a good look at the green end railings, ladder and splash guards which were the standard prior to adoption of silver for these items. The splash guards were not original equipment. The yellow paint scheme likely showed splash dirt on the ends more than the original red scheme. Black steps replaced the yellow versions on the prototype car shown on the previous page. *Gene Huddleston*

Another good look at end details of a C&O caboose is provided by this view of 90335 taken at Russell, Kentucky, in 1970. The fresh silver paint is a contrast to the green presented in the photo above. In the background is 90337, the two cars separated by a pair of B&O scale test cars. This car has the reflectorized markers, which are shown in the retracted position. It also has the long-handle extension hanging just to the right of the ladder for turning the angle cock. *Gene Huddleston*

Although it is shown in fresh paint, 90031 exhibits two painting peculiarities. The **C&O** monogram is smaller than specified and there is no red side stripe. That possibly indicates the car was painted at a shop that normally did not do a lot of caboose painting. If you look closely it can be seen that all of the rivet heads on the end have been painted silver. Apparently the painter had a little too much time on his hands. **C&O** took this photo at Toledo in November 1968. *C&OHS collection*

149

The first of the seven refurbished ex-Western Maryland cabooses poses for builder photos in early 1966. One end window was sealed on this end due to the application of a clothes locker on the interior. This car has the typical C&O reflectorized markers installed on the ends. This is another example of a caboose painted in the mid-1960s which was not given a red side stripe. *Dwight Jones collection*

C&O 90665, the last of the four experimental steel conversion cabooses of the 1950s, is shown at Peru, Indiana, on September 7, 1959, about three months after being modified from a wood caboose to a steel caboose with a wide-vision cupola. On this original paint scheme the number was on the bottom of the carbody sides. A later era photo in chapter 10 shows the number on the sides of the cupola and the double donut C&O monogram on the bottom of the sides. This car today survives on display at Huntington, West Virginia, at the Collis P. Huntington railroad museum in west Huntington. Notice how the bottom of the cupola end windows are angled to maximize viewing. *James F. EuDaly*

C&O A915 is shown in fresh paint at Peru, Indiana, on August 1, 1971. The car had been painted at Huntington in April 1971 as part of a major program to upgrade older first generation steel (and wood) cabooses. This car models the fluorescent red side stripe which rarely is seen in photos because it faded away quickly, as it is starting to do on this car, only four months out of the paint shop. *collection of Dwight Jones*

150   Steel Cabooses of the Chesapeake & Ohio

This photo of the 3557 gives a good look at the blue roof and shows the reflectorized red stripes applied to the ends of the roof. The cab is shown at Shelby, Kentucky, on December 1, 1971, bringing up the markers on a coal train. *Everett N. Young*

Below, 3583 exhibits a weathered edition of the blue scheme at Walbridge, Ohio, in July 1978. *Everett N. Young*

C&O 3322 is shown on display below. Does that number ring any bells? Yes, it was the cab selected to be the first caboose painted Chessie System. Coincidence or did someone really like that number? Chessie yellow went on this car about one year later.

On display at Huntington, West Virginia, probably in late 1971, is caboose 3322 which shows no evidence of being placed in service yet. The two young models actually were secretaries in the offices at the adjacent C&O depot. The blue banners they are wearing read "Miss Sound Transportation". A sign mounted next to the caboose backup whistle reads "Hey Kids Blow The Toot-Toot". Displayed behind this caboose is what appears to be the old C&O display caboose 90382, brought out for comparison purposes to this new car.[23] *Larry K. Fellure*

151

A string of brand new International Car wide-vision cabooses was photographed shortly after delivery to the railroad. These cars were painted with two coats of exterior single color enamel paint, Pittsburgh Plate Glass Company color # UC-41489 Enchantment Blue. The interior was to receive two coats of single color Pittsburgh Plate Glass enamel paint color # 25954 Vista Green. Floors were to receive one coat of Glidden Company Polyurethane S.G. clear floor coat #37. Exterior lettering consisted of 38" size C&O monograms of # 3271 Yellow Scotchlite material. Exterior numbers also were of Yellow Scotchlite. The roof aprons were to be painted yellow and were specified to be given 3" Red Scotchlite stripes. Yellow roof ends clearly display the 3M Scotchlite red diagonal stripes in this end view. The number of this caboose appears to be the 3183. *C&OHS Collection*

This was the original railroad rendition of what a Chessie-painted caboose would look like. One of the C&O wide vision cabooses was selected as a member of the special PR train that was displayed throughout Chessie System territory to introduce the new image. Ironically, caboose 3238 never was painted into the Chessie System scheme and was the next-to-the-last blue caboose on CSX, being sold in 2010 (see page 130). *C&OHS collection*

C&O 3322, the first Chessie-painted caboose, sits outside the Huntington paint shop in September 1972. When cabooses were painted into the Chessie scheme stencils were used to apply the lettering after the yellow dried. The author's close-up inspection of this car revealed that the blue was applied first then stick-on lettering masks were applied and then the yellow was added. When the masks were removed the lettering was razor sharp. This was the normal painting process for locomotives. *C&OHS collection*

Fresh from the shops, C&O A989 poses in the bright sunshine at Lansing, Michigan. The painters apparently had to make their own stencil for the "A" in the road number. Not only the window frames but also the window sash was painted vermilion on the side body windows. This car is believed to have been painted at Grand Rapids in October 1977, although no stencilled paint date was applied. *Gene Huddleston*

153

In the summer of 1975 the A907 was photographed at Parsons Yard in Columbus, Ohio. This car exhibits the no-frills "Walbridge Scheme", applied to several older cabooses during this era. Although a Chess-C emblem was part of the scheme, the C&O initials and road number digits are of the older Futura Demibold font. *Art Markeley*

A fully reconditioned 90229 is shown at Walbridge, Ohio, on September 14, 1980. The car had been released from the Grand Rapids shops just days earlier. New FRA windows highlight the upgraded exterior appearance. *Dwight Jones*

Baywindow caboose 904141 represents the last group of new cabooses purchased by the C&O. It is shown at Grand Rapids, Michigan, on May 28, 1983. These were the only C&O cabooses to have white safety appliances. *Dwight Jones*

154   Steel Cabooses of the Chesapeake & Ohio

Red 3282 was the first C&O caboose to be painted as a safety slogan caboose. In its renumbered "90" version, the car is on display at Parsons Yard in Columbus on July 10, 1982. The display was part of a safety outing for local employees and their families. *Dwight Jones*

Blue 3246 is shown on the Mosel cab track on the east end of Parsons Yard on June 5, 1976. *Dwight Jones*

Orange 903287 has been through a recent chemical washing and renumbering and is pictured on the light side cab track at Russell on October 24, 1982. *Dwight Jones*

155

In this undated photo, 3287 models its original scheme prior to being renumbered. *collection of Dwight Jones*

The Huntington shops did a nice job painting the Ohio Division safety slogan cabooses. The repainting included applying the body color paint to the midget electric markers as well. Green 3285 is shown on the Mosel caboose track at Columbus on June 5, 1976. *Dwight Jones*

In August of 1977 a rather interesting string of cabooses with diverse paint schemes was being switched at Parsons Yard in Columbus. From left to right, blue safety caboose 3246, red safety caboose 3282, yellow 3539, blue 3275, yellow 3197, and wood 90979 wearing the Walbridge scheme. *Larry McNutt*

156   Steel Cabooses of the Chesapeake & Ohio

The first caboose to be painted as a safety slogan caboose for the Michigan Division was 3664, which then was assigned to service in Canada. This photo was taken at Grand Rapids as the car was being readied to return to service. *C&O Grand Rapids Shops photo, collection of Dwight Jones*

Orange 3664 was photographed on the caboose track at St. Thomas, Ontario, on August 10, 1983, with eight years of road grime and weathering. The car is still wearing its midget electric marker lights but now also has a flashing FRA light mounted to the end of the roof. *Dwight Jones*

This original scheme of 3143 was applied at Grand Rapids in November 1976. The scheme lasted less than five years. This photo was made at Chicago on October 17, 1978. *John Eagan, Jr.*

157

Wearing its second safety slogan paint scheme, which featured yellow ends and yellow side lettering, C&O 3143 is shown at Grand Rapids on July 3, 1982. The Grand Rapids shop applied this second scheme in June 1981. It appears that the shop personnel decided to improve the first scheme with some customizations on this more attractive second version. *Dwight Jones*

The last of the C&O safety slogan cabooses was the 3163, painted at Grand Rapids in December of 1976. This photo was taken prior to release of the car back to active service. Paint color was described as Gold in official company documents. *Grand Rapids Shops photo, collection of Dwight Jones*

This overhead view of the 903287 provides a good look at the roof, which was painted silver on safety cabooses. The car was photographed at Clifton Forge, Virginia, on July 31, 1984. *Douglas B. Nuckles*

158　　　　　　　　　　　　　　　　　　　　　　　　　　　　　　　　　　　　Steel Cabooses of the Chesapeake & Ohio

Caboose 903180 was the last cab to be painted as an operational safety slogan caboose. Details of this project can be found in the chapter covering safety cabooses. The view above shows the car at the end of the C&O Historical Society Columbus, Ohio, Conference on July 25, 1993. The car returned to service at Columbus wearing this scheme for a few weeks. In compliance with CSX wishes, the lettering on the car was adjusted by the author to replace the Chessie markings with those of CSX. The revised lettering version is represented by the below photo of the opposite side of the caboose taken on August 26, 1993. Later, at the request of local Columbus officers, the author replaced the CSX safety lantern graphic with the C&O Business Unit logo. This car gave up its longtime Columbus assignment in early 2010 and took up local assignment at Fostoria, Ohio. *both, Dwight Jones*

Below, Chessie Mechanical Department draftsmen prepared a painting and lettering drawing for each of the safety slogan cabooses even using crayons to accurately color the drawings. *C&O Historical Society collection*

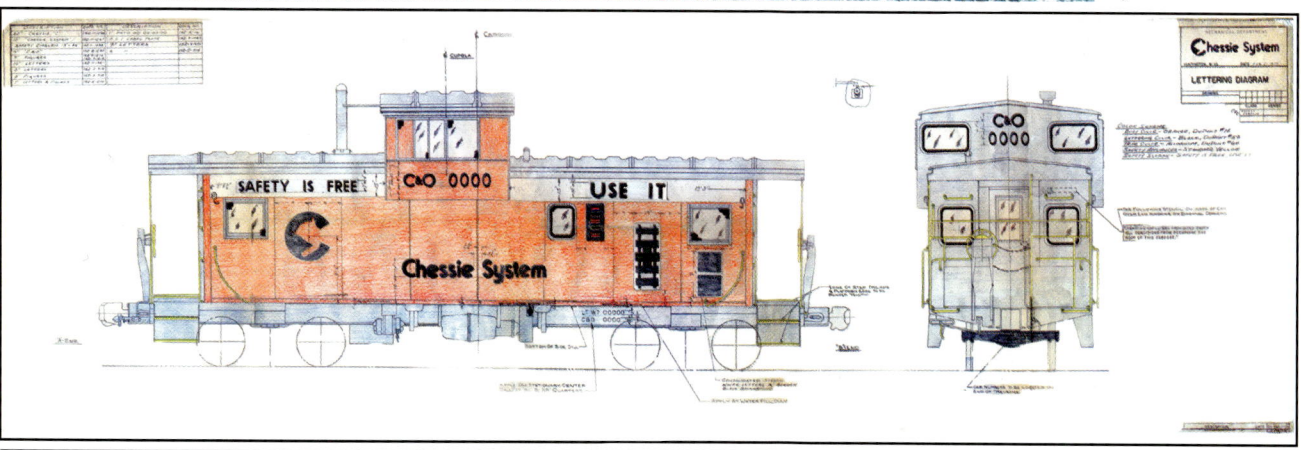

159

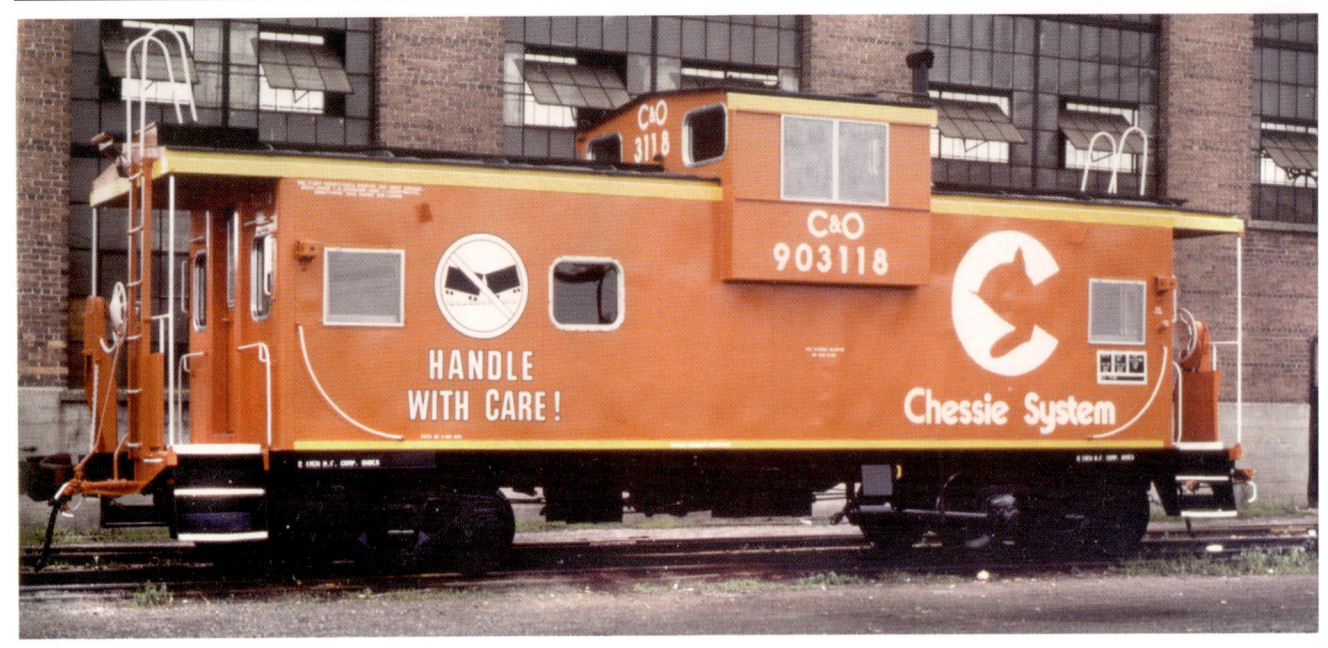

The first caboose to be painted as a Careful Car Handling caboose was 903118, shown at the Grand Rapids shops on July 3, 1982. The car was being held to await inspection by company officers prior to completion of two other cars at Grand Rapids. *Dwight Jones*

This overhead view of 903118 provides a good look at the Enchantment Blue roof applied to these CCH cabooses. On September 18, 1982, 903118 was trailing a westbound manifest departing Russell, Kentucky. *Dwight Jones*

Four honest-to-goodness "red" cabooses were added to the C&O caboose roster with acquisition of the Toledo Terminal Railroad in 1984. It did not take long for the cars to be relettered C&O, as shown by TT #91, wearing its new owner's 903327 number at Toledo on February 23, 1985. *Dwight Jones*

160　　　　　　　　　　　　　　　　　　　　　　　　　　　　　　　　Steel Cabooses of the Chesapeake & Ohio